QUEERCORE
HOW TO PUNK A REVOLUTION: AN ORAL HISTORY

Editors: Liam Warfield, Walter Crasshole,
and Yony Leyser

Introduction: Anna Joy Springer
and Lynn Breedlove

Queercore: How to Punk a Revolution: An Oral History
Liam Warfield, Walter Crasshole, and Yony Leyser © 2021
Vaginal Davis interview passages by and courtesy of Philipp Meinert.
This edition © PM Press

ISBN: 978-1-62963-796-9 (paperback)
ISBN: 978-1-62963-820-1 (ebook)
Library of Congress Control Number: 2019946104

Cover design by John Yates/www.stealworks.com
Interior design by briandesign

10 9 8 7 6 5 4 3 2

PM Press
PO Box 23912
Oakland, CA 94623
www.pmpress.org

Printed in the USA

CONTENTS

EXTREMELY FORWARD INTRODUCTION
BY LYNN BREEDLOVE AND ANNA JOY SPRINGER

Anna Joy Springer and Lynn Breedlove

AJ: Hey! This might be our first collaboration! Except the five-plus years we spent together. Which started at the Tribe 8/Blatz meeting about the cover of that first split 7" we were on.

LB: Love is political action.

AJ: True. But we haven't been together in twenty-five years. Unless you count our friendship. Which I've always believed is the model for lesbian post-breakup feminist family.

LB: EX-tended family.

AJ: Sad to discover it's rare to hate someone you love, then keep loving them as a BFF for twenty-five years after the fallout.

LB: And now that we don't take ourselves so seriously, we get to make each other laugh till our eyelids turn inside out.

AJ: And talk about the Goddess.

LB: So much for cool.

AJ: But, really, so many people in this oral history were somehow part of your and my story. Except those mansplainy guys. But they are represented here too, for those who love them.

LB: Someone's gotta do it.

AJ: All touched some, and some touched all. Like Iraya Robles of Sta-Prest and organizer at Epicenter and QTip, and Miriam Klein-Stahl. And Sister Spit. Enough for a whole other book.

LB: You write, I'll snark.

AJ: This book, though. Frankly, I thought, surely, it might be kind of enraging, before I read it. I was like, "If Adele Bertei isn't mentioned in the first few pages, I'm not gonna read it." But yay, she is.

LB: Don't call me Shirley. But tell me more.

AJ: Adele Bertei, queer punk musician extraordinaire of The Contortions and The Bloods in the Lower East Side NYC queer punk wildness times, before homocore and parallel to the fancy cocaine club scene. Lives around the corner from me in LA, a gold record in her bathroom.

LB: There was so much more going on in the '70s and '80s than I knew, besides RuPaul living in a park as a nonbinary pink-mohawked teen. I claimed we were the first all-out, punk dyke band. Always lying.

AJ: Me too. Except when I say that one of my favorite stories here is how Popstitutes (probably) made that 1989 gay parade float, the cop car squashed by a giant high heel, and they were handing out heels and baseball bats to beat the cop car. That's where Justin Vivian Bond met up with Silas and Leslie and Diet and all these incredible people! That, and lesbian theater at the Rhino.

LB: I was extremely high somewhere. I missed that, the White Night Riot, Fab Mab, everything. Blanks need filling in for those who were not born yet, too little, or too checked out.

AJ: I'd just graduated high school in Merced. And you definitely did not miss the amazing parts. You were one of the main attractions. Too bad we're all hurling toward the next abyss now.

LB: Lighten up, will ya, Professor?

AJ: As someone who is extremely skeptical of "let's pretend this isn't a hierarchy," I do tend to mention misogyny, environmental collapse, and systemic racism more than people like. But they gave me a whole section here to rail.

LB: Careening between awareness and action, fights and apologies.

AJ: Justin Vivian Bond gave one of my favorite quotes about that: "I have failings in my own consciousness, in my own habits, and what we used to see as humorous is totally unacceptable now." So generous and elegant, like she has always been, before and after Broadway. What a great model for us to use today, to admit the truth without defensiveness or blame! Maybe you're right: this history is a roadmap. So glad none of us had Twitter back then.

LB: Social media would have overwhelmed us. But instead . . . meet me at the merch table and let's talk/hug/fuck it out. Or if people gave your band side-eye, you'd just wonder why. Now we can access online tomes about what to do different, fail at, learn from, while discerning selfcare from narcissism.

AJ: On a good day. We had rules though, like *No talking shit about dyke bands*. Cypher borrowed it from Tribe 8.

LB: Our rule was about chick bands. So Lilith Fair got a pass. Just as it's not a boycott if you never use it anyway, it's not service if it doesn't make you puke a little.

AJ: And *No fucking anyone in the band*. That made the orgy birthday party guest lists challenging.

LB: A panicky-at-play-parties ex–speed freak, I found safe spaces at snack tables and smoking areas. Anyway, there we were, disrupters of the disruption, making out on the iffy couch, beyond the sweaty sold out Bikini Kill show, soundtrack to our fluorescent-lit world. (Although I wondered, why can't we be popular? Castration and blowjobs are as charming as girls in short skirts yelling "girls to the front!")

AJ: At Klub Kommotion. We'd just gotten together. You helped me move into Shred of Dignity House at 666 Illinois, a queer anarchist collective of organizers, artists, technicians, rabble rousers—I couldn't believe I'd get to live there.

LB: Queen of punk. Why not?

AJ: I'm not big on the monarchy.

LB: You slid right into the SF homocore scene.

AJ: Standing on a ladder in my 1940s dress and tool belt and hairy legs and no deodorant, installing the neon sign I'd made for Silas Howard and Harry Dodge's Red Dora's The Bearded Lady Truckstop cafe.

LB: If you don't like the scene, grab a hammer and make one of your own.

AJ: I was always so busy and freaked out. School, the Gr'ups, the peepshow, neon, a girlfriend with DID [dissociative identity disorder]. She developed AIDS and killed herself just a few weeks before the protease inhibitor cocktails came out. Fucking awful.

LB: I should have been more empathetic. But death was all around me, from bike messengering, homoing, or dope fiending. I saw it and kept moving, while bonding over grief. Once a self-centered bastard, always a lovable jerk.

AJ: I get it. I'd first met Silas, you, and Leslie after our split record came out when you guys were on tour with MDC in Europe. We all met at a meeting to try to fix the mess of our ignorantly fucked up split 7" that'd already been distributed. Blatz members, including me, had no idea how not-in-a-good-way rude it was.

LB: *Now* you tell me.

AJ: Tribe 8 was right to say two bands with no South African black members, or any African American members, or trans women, should *not* use documentary South African black transgender slow dancing photographs from midcentury Apartheid as a representative and delightful cover image, or that the long ramble from the record-label guy about how American blues (which he related to whatever music must have been playing in those documentary photos) was really just another way to package a queer record with no songs about anything in the photos or about the blues.

LB: Mahia, Leslie, and Silas spearheaded that. I was Rip Van Winkle, awake after a long slumber, lucky to be in a band where I got caught up to speed by people of color and the working class, who, as usual, did all the emotional labor.

AJ: Right. I was the working-class feminist on the Blatz side of things, trying to keep up. And most people don't know half of Blatz was queer. One member couldn't be out because he was a Vietnam vet and could lose his benefits. After two or three meetings about cultural appropriation as racism, we pulled the records, got a new label and a new cover, which I drew with my ex, who was still alive then. I never finished it, so the woman in the foreground should be sitting on a pillow, but instead seems just to be hovering . . .

LB: Floatation device ancestor homos, here/not here.

AJ: That meeting was the big pivot, where I saw I was more like the members of Tribe 8 than Blatz. I could seem not crazy for noticing hypocrisy and ignorance under the banner of anti-political correctness. That's also where I crushed on you. So butch in your leather pants, but crying and telling Cat, your first drummer, "If you don't shut up, I'm gonna punch you."

LB: We were processing so earnestly about really crucial shit, and she kept yelling, "Core of my asshole!"

AJ: Enraging. But I loved that you could be such a boy and also PMS during a feminist meeting about representations of race in punk.

LB: That slip was usually more appropriately funneled into my budding onstage persona of blowfish dissonance. Homocore meant that rejected by outsiders, we colored inside new lines we'd just learned to draw, laughing at "anarchy! no rules!" But boundaries are crucial in chaos.

Punk's main rule: NO MAKING OUT AT THE SHOW, NO LOVE, NO ROMANCE, NO SEX. We perceived that as some counterrevolutionary shit; our paths diverged. Some people *did* need to stop thinking with their dicks. We needed to *start* thinking with ours. So we loaded bags of silicon into vans, arguing with feminists: Is stage diving male behavior? What if femmes/queers/trans, fistfuck while crowd surfing. Did that happen? Was it physically impossible? If it's a myth, promote that lie, make quistory. No, really, make it up.

AJ: But I never thought the "not having a sexuality" thing was part of punk at all. I loved The Yeastie Girlz, and as we said in Blatz, "the Ashtray's just a petting zoo." Meaning lots of tweaking and fucking on beer-pee floors. So gross/so hot. I love how the book starts with nightmare genderfuck monsters wrecking nerves for fun, instead of sad little shame spirals in our own kitchens. reconfiguring emotional history, fun and tragedy in the same space, through swirls of hysterical ecstatic contagion, dead-serious operatic, grotesque absurdism articulated by contributors to this history. I'd never heard how the Toronto homocore scene was a "faction" till I read this. I was not a zine reader. I had heard of *Fertile La Toyah Jackson*. Luckily, a lot of the zines mentioned are now online and in paper archives. I love when Sarah Schulman expounds on zines and papers that informed punk and queerpunk zines. And theatricality in AIDS activism and bands.

LB: Zines! At every show I got handed three. *Bamboo Girl* by Sabrina Margarita Alcantara-Tan was one of Tribe 8's faves. And Diseased Pariah News, a compilation by people with HIV/AIDS. Facing death? Make a joke. Time honored tradition of the traumatized and targeted.

AJ: People in the same room, transforming each other—different from sending digital notes with an audience of invisible watchers. The power of physical proximity, leaving the house, meeting people outside the Mini-Herd.

LB: Band name!

AJ: Reading about the anarchist gathering where Deke and Tom met, I got misty. I'd meet people accidentally, at shows, or from flyers on cafe walls.

LB: Phone poles! That OCD self-appointed pole-cleaning gay, with his X-Acto knife in the Castro. I'd yell, *"Dude! That's our bulletin board.* Give it a rest." He finally did. RIP.

AJ: But I wish I had known about the SPEW convention and Homocore Chicago. I know Cypher did at least one gig at Fireside Bowl.

LB: Bowling and queercore, together at last. I remember Joanne and Carolyn and Mark, founders of Homocore Chicago, greeting us in their living room where we laid down our gear. They treated us like royalty, a van fulla studded-up dykes, POC, femmes, genderfuckers, kickin' ass for the working class, who barely got through middle America intact, recognized as helpful geniuses. A homecoming.

AJ: But sometimes I was so upset because of stuff happening in our relationship . . .

LB: I spent a lotta time in the van crying . . .

AJ: . . . which took place when both of us were on tour, and then I'd get to these venues all over the US and Europe and see Tribe 8 posters, and I'd be proud of you and also braggy and also mad because I was monogamous and you weren't, and that broke my old-fashioned girl heart.

LB: I did like finding your punny love poems addressed to me in silver Sharpie all over Chi Town and New Orleans.

AJ: I loved leaving you notes on tour in venue bathrooms. Still, I hated that people thought of Cypher in the Snow as "Tribe 8's Girlfriends." So now I'd like to claim for history that you guys were our girlfriends. Boyfriends. And that Cypher was a phenomenal band and deserves a whole book of its own.

LB: My name is Lynn Breedlove, and I approve this message.

AJ: Like for instance, how beautiful were the members of Cypher? Remember Ulla McKnight? And Daniela Sea, Dorothy Wang, Carmen White, La La Hulse, Chloe Sherman, Margaret Hitchcock, Elitrea Frye, and Rusten Menard? Cypher sounded queer, like creepy circus self-help party time, all off kilter. We're all still doing so many cool queer punk things. Which leads me to a small critique of this book: It kind wraps the whole queercore thing up in the past at the end, like oral history documentary things do so often.

LB: Punk is loose ends. Quit tying us up. Unless it's consensual.

AJ: But like I said in my rage-oration after the East Bay punk documentary in Hollywood, we are not done. Old is not over, or stupid.

LB: It's adding *A* for asexual to the unpronounceable acronym. Buying Les-baru soccer dad SUVs to play for the six people of fifty, who said they were interested/going on Facebook but were too screen-drained to leave the couch.

AJ: And an asterisk for so many unimaginable ways of being queer we have yet to know, as we grind away at systems that keep sexist, antiqueer, normative, white-supremacist, antifreak, empire-building, warmonger-ing, earth-killing practices at the mythical center of "common decency." With humour and style. Punk didn't end when it dyed its hair a "natural" shade.

LB: Black is a color. Brown is a color. Gray. Add them to the queermo flag.

AJ: And can we stop acting like our art and interventions have an expi-ration date? It freaks me out when people from "the old days" say the scene is dead, while right in the middle of it, people of color, trans folks, and other targeted peoples make big splashes.

LB: Fuck You Pay Us, Squid Ink, G.L.O.S.S., Against Me, Trap Girl. Sarchasm, Cristy C. Road's Choked Up.

AJ: So many bands, all over the country and the world. I love how Deke pushes back against that notion of punk being dead ("It just smells like it is!") at the end. Punk is a stretched-out pantyhose, with lots and lots of elasticity still. It may smell of grandma foot, it may have a hole . . .

LB: Ageism is dead!

AJ: . . . full of discharge, dope, and Hallmark bunnies, but still a cathe-dral full of raging freaks who love wrongly and gloriously, a prismatic panty hose.

LB: Boundary! No unicorn puke.

AJ: I wish I had time to talk about what all the Riot Crrrones are up to now.

LB: Hag crusties!

AJ: Hey, remember when you and I took your mom out for her birthday to see Kiki and Herb at Eichelberger's in SF, and afterward Justin Vivian and your mom looked like twins and ignored us, smoking at the bar the whole night?

LB: And talked endlessly about Jackie Kennedy and Chanel suits, fell in love, and admired each other from afar in femme solidarity forever.

AJ: And that time we went to New York and stayed at Elitrea's squat, and we went with Chloe Transister to the Jayne County show, and then to that drag punk disco place.

LB: Don Hill's.

AJ: To see Misstress Formika aka Michael Formika Jones, who gave us free dinner at that De Sade themed restaurant, La Nouvelle Justine, where servers crawled to the table with plates on their back . . .

LB: And she was the dominatrix maître d', which made me love her even more than when she shredded an extra-large Tribe 8 shirt and braided it up the sides into a minidress before jumping onstage to introduce us, and then lounged in the laps of half-naked hunks in the basement. As you were saying, Justine's?

AJ: I beat one of the New York Hags on the whipping post by the bar.

LB: And Marilyn Manson waved at us from another table, and we were all, "Whoa. They know who we are." You could order perversions off the menu: your date's dinner from a dog dish, in a cage, on a leash! Straight rich people, but also trans women in Catholic schoolgirl dresses, lined up to get spanked by goth drag queens, who treated us poor punks special.

AJ: And I heard Apocalyptica for the first time. So sweet. *Such* good service!

LB: I felt super high. And confused. And happy. This was *it*.

AJ: And remember hugging Vag at the shows she put on in LA at that punk club, and how giant and magnificent and sweaty and friendly she was, like genuinely not stuck up at all, even though she was *such* a worldmaker?

LB: A mythical superhero in whose arms you'd be cradled, snatched from the jaws of monsters.

AJ: For realsies. I just learned about Cholita in this book.

LB: Her eponymous comedy routine was a crackup.

AJ: I also discovered G.B. Jones's first zine was called *Hide*. That's a good thing to do sometimes, achieve a certain safety that's not enforced invisibility, but agency. Who's peeping what, when, how.

LB: Hide and seek. Jump out from behind a couch! Then disappear.

AJ: Visibility is not a perfect 24/7 solution. I like that the participants in this book acknowledge a million ways of engaging, feelings, *inver*-sections, perverse politics. The strategies move and grow like a slime mold.

LB: Ew. Slime mold! Always chasing people with slugs. Remember when you made Cypher paper dolls, tracing your whole-body outlines on the wall, and Chloe Sherman photographed your Lunachicks fuck-you-don't-objectify-me thing and made it dykey? I was all, Noooo. Make us cute! They already think we're gross! And you insisted, Nope. We're gross! And scary!

AJ: Viscosity. The overlapping slimy ecospheres of us. Slugs, rivers, scenes, cultures, unnamed outsiders and girly-girls. And this book gets that notion. The emphasis, neither individualistic nor anti-individual is on inevitable friction, upsetting, ecstatic and/or generative. It maps that approach. Except Bruce should have apologized to G.B., instead of just saying he should have credited her.

LB: Go beyond "sorry." Acknowledge you fucked up, say you're working on it. Although no one will believe it until you do.

AJ: Credit people, especially if they're marginalized. That's a good rule. Also, don't wear swastika anything. It's never cute. Or the fucking

Confederate flag. Or the US flag. Unless it's mangled and matches the dead couch. Any other rules, or pertinent folk songs?

LB: Rule number one: no swastikas.
Rule number two: See rule number one.
Shortest punk song ever:
"Is it OK to punch Nazis?"
"Yes!"
by Commando.
(sequel to; "Is heroin vegan?"
"Yes!"
by Fly)

AJ: Just because it's vegan doesn't mean it's a healthy supplement. But this book is. And tasty. Read up!

LB: Yep. Unless you are ADD and have a reader. In which case, collaborate on an audiobook. Oral oral history—what could be more queer?

AJ: It's surprisingly good. These punk histories are usually so boring and narrow.

LB: All the depth and breadth.

AJ: This is absolutely the place to talk about orals and size. Also, come find us, it's easy.

LB: If the CIA knows our dreams and every whisper, why not our pals?

AJ: No stamps required.

AJ and LB: Yeah! Look up people you discover here! And also find out about Raquel Gutierrez, Joan Jett Blakk, Iraya Robles, Diet Popstitute, Leslie Mah, Valerie Stadler, Stacey/Stacie Quijas, Michelle Tea, Ivy Jeanne McClelland, M Lamar, Juba Kalamka, Tae Won Yu, Sini Anderson, Erica Dawn Lyle, Tara Jane O'Neil, Danny Levesque, Samara Halpern, Leon Mostovoy, Rachel Carnes, Josh Ploeg, Christopher Lee, Sarah Kirsch, Chloe Dzubilo, Waiyde Palmer, and definitely The Hags, which was not a band but a gang. Search for queercore bands, zines, books, films, and art. These will hook you into so many others.

AJ: Remember, everyone reading and writing *about* this book also creates and expands queercore mythology. "Where are they now?" Those of us who haven't died? Right here.

LB: If you're tuned in, you may see the dead are also here. Nothing essential is ever lost.

AJ: More love stories! Can I get a "gaymen"?

LB: Hallelujah and pass the ammunition.

INTRODUCTION
BY LIAM WARFIELD

The New Testament would have us believe that *in the beginning was the Word*, but history suggests that the naming of things, whether moments or movements, tends to lag far behind the fact of their existence. Queers and punks have always been with us, under various guises and nearly always on the margins, and the two have long intersected and cross-pollinated.

Before its musical application, as Bruce LaBruce notes, *punk* was jail-house slang for a guy who took it up the ass. But the word is much older, dating at least as far back as Shakespeare, and has referred, over time, to prostitutes, delinquents, cowards, and conditions of poor health (*feeling punk*). *Queer* has a similarly amorphous history: first appearing as a sort of shorthand for anything odd, perverse, eccentric or otherworldly; later as a slur along the lines of *fairy* or *fag*; reclaimed in the 1980s by activists and academics and more recently in vogue as an LGBTQI catchall. In a sense, the two words have been fellow-travelers through time, shifting from terms of derision to badges of otherness to popular acceptance and near-meaninglessness.

Any starting point, then, is going to be arbitrary; for the purposes of this book I date the *queer punk* phenomenon to 1969. Neither term then had quite come into its modern usage, but in many ways '69 was a moment of conception for the movement-to-be. The Stonewall riots, of course, marked the coming-out of the righteous queen and the gay liberationist, outrageous and confrontational, into the public sphere—queer in all but name. The year 1969 might be less obviously a punk touchstone, but between Altamont and Charles Manson, the Days of Rage and the Weather Underground, debut albums by The Stooges and MC5 and the stirrings of glam, it's clear that something punk was in the air. Elsewhere on the fringes, John Waters's first feature film, *Mondo*

Trasho, and Jackie Curtis's play *Femme Fatale*, starring future punk icons Wayne/Jayne County and Patti Smith, melded cheap drag and shock theatrics with a crass and caustic sense of humor that was very much queer-punk avant la lettre.

By the time punk was named and codified, in the mid-to-late 1970s, countercultural expressions of gender and sexuality had become more complex and ambivalent. Punk, as a matter of course, dismissed, devalued and deprogrammed sex—the body itself was chopped, screwed, pierced, tattooed, a site of conflict and opposition. It almost goes without saying that the first waves of punk—in New York, London, LA, and elsewhere—were queer to a high degree. If one believes half the stories told by trans/punk pioneer Jayne County, *everyone* on the early scene at least fooled around with sex and gender. Some, like the Germs' Darby Crash, were more closeted than others—though it didn't take a genius to read between the lines of songs like "Sex Boy" and "American Leather." Others, like Nervous Gender and the Screamers, were about as unambiguous as could be.

It's tempting to attribute the birth of queercore proper, in the mid-1980s, to a nexus of circumstances and influences: Reagan, Thatcher and the rise of neoliberalism; the blood-politics of the AIDS epidemic; and an identity crisis for punk rock, as scenes which had begun as havens for weirdos, women and queer malcontents were overrun with skinheads and jocks. But unlike most other punk creation stories, in which seminal scenes seem to spring, fully formed and almost inevitable, out of particular cultural climates—New York's exploding downtown, class strife and general unrest in mid-1970s London, the total banality of late-1970s Los Angeles—queercore began more as an absence than a confluence.

What was a queer punk to do, in mid-1980s Toronto? Aside from a handful of artier bands and provocative fanzines, the punk scene was macho, hardcore, traditionalist. Meanwhile the gay world wanted nothing to do with punk rock—you could hardly *dance* to it, and it didn't sell drinks. For G.B. Jones, Bruce LaBruce and their small coterie of artists, musicians and freaks, there were a couple of places to meet: an all-night restaurant called Just Desserts and a dive bar called Together's, where they would show experimental films and occasionally host bands—hardly the makings of a legendary scene.

So they did what visionaries do—they *made up* a scene and fooled other people into believing in it. Borrowing generously from Warhol on the one hand and the Situationists on the other, Bruce, G.B., and their collaborators spread the illusion, through bands, films, and their influential zine *J.D.s* (that would be juvenile delinquents, James Dean, or J.D. Salinger—take your pick) that there was this queer punk *explosion* happening in Toronto. The word *homocore* first appeared as a wise-crack neologism in the pages of *J.D.s*, meant to take the piss out of the hypermasculine hardcore punk scene. A flippant fuck-you to the staid punk world or an international call-to-arms? In the Bay Area, where queer punk had been percolating for some time, Tom Jennings and Deke Nihilson borrowed *homocore* for their zine of the same name, which quickly graduated to newsprint and a print run of thousands. By the early 1990s, the term of preference had shifted to the more inclusive *queercore*, and the banner was being raised by bands, zine-writers and malcontents all over the map.

Queercore, it should be said, was not simply a hybrid, a mashup of disparate genres like rap-metal or folk-rock. If anything, the queer-punk stance was reductive rather than additive, defined largely in the negative, the stripped-away. *We didn't fit here and we didn't fit there* is a common refrain throughout the narrative—*freaks among the freaks*, as Jody Bleyle says. Nor was it simply a musical movement, though it was certainly that. *The amazing thing about queercore is that it was not just zines, not just music*, notes G.B. Jones, one of the movement's progenitors. *There was film, there was photography, there was artwork, there was writing, perfor-mance art—pretty much every medium was incorporated into queercore.*

Why an oral history? The easy answer is that this project fell into my lap; my friend Yony Leyser, a filmmaker based in Berlin, had amassed nearly a hundred hours of interviews with over fifty movers and shakers from the queercore cosmos, and after cramming as much as possible into a ninety-minute documentary, he had a rich trove of unused mate-rial that he thought I might like to turn into a book.

To my surprise, there was not a whole lot of existing literature on the subject. There were mountains of primary-source documents, of course: the thousands of zines that constituted the "queer zine explo-sion" of the late 1980s and '90s, many of them lovingly archived and easily accessible, others gathering dust in closets and basements—not to mention all the tapes, records, films, videos, photographs, flyers, and other ephemera of the time. But queercore as a cultural phenomenon has, for the most part, resisted the box-set treatment—the gallery shows, zine anthologies, anniversary tours, and coffee-table books that might signify the movement's official passing into history. A 2012 article in *Out* magazine brought together some of the scene's best-known figures for a quick overview; the first book-length critical treatment of the subject was released just a few years ago, by an eminent university press; and queercore—as a catchphrase, at least—has made a few odd, if not surprising, forays into mainstream consciousness (e.g. *Queercore*, the line of Gucci luxury shoes that debuted in 2017). There's sure to be more on the way—our culture requires endless grist for its nostalgia mills, and even what was dangerously cutting-edge a quarter century ago tends to be marketable over time. *Capitalism*, as artist and filmmaker Scott Treleaven puts it, *eventually digests everything*.

That said, the obvious virtue of oral history is that it allows the protagonists to tell their own stories in their own voices (the editor's scissors and paste aside). It can be an especially messy mode of storytelling: the narrators may not always be reliable, they may embellish, gloss over, half-remember, or contradict. But history is messy, and punk is messy; and I'd like to hope that the multitude of voices in this book, brought into cacophonous discourse, are able to animate their subject in ways that a tidier telling might not.

I wrap things up around 1999 not simply because thirty years makes a nice, round figure, but because by the cusp of the millennium various cultural and technological forces were challenging many of the basic premises around which queercore operated. What was the point of a photocopied zine when information could be shared so easily, and in so many ways, online? Why form a band when a laptop could just as easily light up the party? In his film, *Queercore: How to Punk a Revolution*, Yony Leyser attempts to chart some of inroads queercore has made into millennial culture—from artists like Peaches and The Gossip, who in the first decade of the twenty-first century employed queercore signifiers while climbing the charts and making the tabloids, to the ascendance of queer hip-hop and trans visibility. For the purposes of this book, I think the story works best with a temporal endpoint—though there's ample musing on today's quandaries, the narrative does not delve into the many bands, zines, festivals, websites, and so on that have carried the torch in the new millennium.

The intention behind this book is not to rehash anyone's glory days. It doesn't pretend to be comprehensive or authoritative or the story *behind* the story. It doesn't set out to describe a template for future revolt or to make a place for unsung heroes in some queer pantheon. It's not meant as a rallying cry to *make a zine!* or *start a band!* It certainly doesn't mean to say *look how far we've come!* Nor do I think that young queer people (or *any* queer people) are duty-bound to learn about their elders or celebrate queer history. History is useful insofar as it interrogates the present—and the present does desperately need some interrogation. Let's hope, then, that the primordial currents of queer and punk continue crossing in new and vital ways.

WRECKING NERVES
STONEWALL TO CBGB (1969–1976)

Jayne County: I have to say, we had a *ball*. We were too young to get into the bars, so we had fake IDs; but really, we made our party on the street. I don't know how we kept from getting murdered, but we did. We used to joke about having two pairs of shoes in our purses, one to prance around in and one to change into and run. Because you had people coming along in cars and yelling at you, *fucking faggot, fucking queer!* . . . and then you had the cops, who

Wayne County and the Backstreet Boys' *At the Trucks!*

wanted to shave your head and put you in jail, call your daddy because you were wearing a dress. It was pretty fucked up, but we managed to have a ball. We had *such* a good time.

We would wreck people's nerves. We'd call each other up—*You going wrecking tonight?* I don't know if I'm in the mood . . .*Well, there's a party. We'll have some free drinks, and then we'll go wrecking*—OK, let's go! We'd put on some lipstick, fluff up our hair, pull our little hip-huggers down and go wrecking. We'd go down to the Fox Theater and have one of those, *can you make it walking around the Fox Theater in high heels?* Your friends would follow in a car, in case people tried to beat you up or kill you or anything. And when you came around the corner they would go, *Yay, she made it, she walked around the Fox Theater on high heels!* That's what we had to do—we couldn't get in the bars, we had to make our own fun.

Another thing we would do, when the clubs would let out we'd see all these straight guys, with girls and all, and we'd slow down the car and go, *Oh!, he's with a* girl *tonight. Do you* believe *that? Miss Thing, oh my god, I sucked his dick last night, honey, it was* horrible! Stuff like that. We'd go down to the Greyhound bus station and go to the men's room, the men would be peeing, and we'd sneak up behind them and go, *Woooh!, look at all the dicks for* sucking, *baby, yeah!*, totally freak them out. That's what we had to do—we just went around wrecking people's damn nerves. And a lot of the closet-case gay people, gay people that were kind of "respectable," would *not* invite us to parties because we would give them away—the neighbors would know it was a *queer party*. And we *would*— we'd go out on the balcony and scream and put on makeup—and before you know it the cops would be pulling around. It was like, *Don't invite* that *group of screaming queens. They will* ruin *your party.*

Penny Arcade: In New York in the late '60s there was this whole pre-cursor to punk, John Vaccaro and Playhouse of the Ridiculous, and it was totally queer. In 1969, Danny Fields brought Iggy Pop to New York. Iggy Pop was exactly our kind of person. There was already this queer, edgy thing going on that was kind of like *rock* without the *roll*, nervy downtown-homo-queer-whatever. I mean, Patti Smith, Debbie Harry, Jayne County, Ruby and The Rednecks—there were all those early punk bands that were all part of that scene, and it was very queer.

I left New York in 1971; I left just when Wayne County was moving from doing DJing at Max's backroom, upstairs, to doing his own music. I ended up going with John Vaccaro to Amsterdam; I could have gone to London with Andy Warhol but I decided not to go because I was really sick of the "Pop Tart" thing—and I was the flavor of the year; I was, like, the it-girl of 1969, and all I saw was that I was getting invited to richer and richer people's houses. The art that we were making wasn't compelling the way it was with John Vaccaro. Vaccaro was hardcore. Vaccaro was like the Rolling Stones to everybody else's Beatles. By the time I came back at the end of 1974, all of these people had started to establish themselves, and the music scene at Max's had kind of started in earnest. In the beginning, it was just, like, once in a while somebody would play at Max's—Lou Reed, Iggy, Alice Cooper—that's pretty much all I remember. I don't think there were a lot of bands that played there before about 1972. But there was always a queer element.

In about 1975, Danny Fields said to me, *You have to come to CBGBs—my band The Ramones are playing!* So I went. It was really hard to see The Ramones as machismo. And even though they were (mostly) hetero, it was really hard to see them as hetero. The downtown scene was a lot queerer, y'know? Nobody was really interested in people's sexuality, unless you personally wanted to fuck the person. And that's how I feel about gender identity. Who gives a fuck what your sexual orientation is? That's so counter-revolutionary, and counter-evolutionary.

Larry Livermore: I got into the first wave of gay liberation starting around '69, right after Stonewall, but at the time I was in Michigan. We had one gay bar in Ann Arbor and it was such a little scene that all the weirdos of every kind, not necessarily gay people, but just every kind of weirdo—in one corner would be one or two leather people, in another corner would be a couple of dykes, and there were these two teenage boys that later became transgender—we didn't call it that back then, but they both had gender surgery later on. In 1971 glam rock arrived, a lot of straight people dressing up like the Dolls and Ziggy Stardust and stuff that would hang out there.

The bar was excluding these black drag queens, and we staged a parade in drag down Main Street. This is a small midwestern town—a liberal midwestern town, but it was still pretty shocking in 1970-something. I was never a drag queen; I think I've been in drag one other time besides that in my life, but it was like, *You're picking on the weirdos. Well, we're the weirdos and you can't do that.* I felt really empowered by that sense that *we don't need to hide anymore,* and that's what homocore was too. It was the same thing. The hippie culture had to have these liberation movements for women and gay people, the punk scene had to do the same thing. Seems kind of weird that they would have to, but that's how it felt.

John Waters: We made *fun* of hippies. Yippies, though, were kind of punks. Yippies went to political *riots.* That was like—my idea of a rave would be a riot. We would just hitchhike to different cities where there was going to be a riot. And I went to get laid and get high—yes, I was against the war in Vietnam, but I was more interested in getting laid and getting high. But part of that *was* fighting the cops, and the tear gas and everything—and it *was* exciting to have sex at a riot! Even though punk wasn't around yet—that *felt* like punk to me.

Jayne County: When I first started getting on stage in the late '60s, people were calling it drag rock. Or gay rock, or transvestite rock. Then the "glam rock" thing kind of stuck. Instead of *drag* or *gay* or whatever, you could say *glam*. It was like with punk, when instead of *punk* people started saying *new wave*—it became whitewashed for the general public.

Mykel Board: I used to go to New York Dolls concerts, down at Club 82. They played often, every couple of weeks. And suddenly they stopped dressing up—suddenly they weren't in dresses anymore. They were playing the same music, the same stuff going on. I asked somebody there, *What's going on? How come they're not dressing up anymore?* And they said, *Don't you know? Glitter is dead. It's punk rock now.* So my first experience of punk rock—this was 1974, '75?—it was the stuff I'd always liked! So, OK, it's *punk rock* now—it has a different name, but it's the same music, same people. Punk rock probably suited my personality more than glitter did because I'm very much of a contrarian, and an *anti-* kind of guy; and punk rock was an *anti-* kind of music.

Jayne County: That first wave of punk that happened, I was the first to play at CBGB. I played there when even it wasn't *called* CBGB, it was called Hilly's and it was nothing but Hells Angels, and I had to walk out on stage in front of an audience of Hells Angels. And they were freaking out, because that was the height of when I was really doing awful stuff—fucking myself with a fake pussy, with a three-headed dildo, masturbating with a statue of the Virgin Mary, eating fake dog food out of a toilet. And surprise, surprise—the Hells Angels loved it. By the end of the night everyone was drunk, and I was sitting in their laps, camping around, and just being totally outrageous. What I was doing was so in-your-face that the Hells Angels loved it. They thought it was fabulous.

Mykel Board: CBGB and Max's Kansas City were the only two venues for punk rock in New York. Jayne County used to play at Max's Kansas City—at that time she was Wayne County. She was completely outrageous, with a big bouffant hairdo and a "Dave Clark Five" tiara, and she would sing songs about eating shit. . . . She inspired a lot of people to do extreme things not only with the music, but with sexuality.

Jayne County: I played Max's more than CBGB, I was really more of a Max's Kansas City act. I mean, I loved CBGB, I have the best memories in the world . . . CBGB, that bathroom down there—you could run down into that bathroom and wait until someone famous came in, that would be your chance to see their cocks. There were no stalls, people had to just stand there and pee, and you could just run and go, *Oooh, I see your cock, yeah!* They'd go, *Here it is, Jayne, come and get it . . .* A lot of them did that to me— David Johansen, Deedee . . . those bathrooms down there, they were fun. People would get drunk and just turn around and whip it out.

An early Wayne (Jayne) County flyer

Quite a few of the punks *were* gay, they just weren't out. They might not even have thought of themselves as gay—a lot of them were very young at the time. I guess everyone knows Walter Lure from The Heartbreakers was . . . he wasn't out either, but he came out as gay in London, during the whole punk thing. Me and my manager, Leee Black Childers, who was also managing The Heartbreakers, we began to notice that every time we saw Walter he was with a pretty boy, somebody that was very noticeably gay. He didn't say anything, he just let people assume what they wanted to assume.

With Joe Strummer from The Clash, there was always the rumor that he was bisexual. I think he was totally gay. At the beginning, when he was with The Clash, he probably didn't know what he was either, he was very young. But he had an affair for *years* with a famous London artist. You always heard rumors about people. And my friend Leee Black Childers, who was on the business side of things—Leee is totally gay, he's a big raving queen. He had gay experiences with a whole list of people and he'd seduce people left and right. We were at a party in London, a lot of the early punks were there . . . and I found myself up on the roof, and I saw this blonde person sitting there, and Leee Black Childers down on his knees, working away . . . and when I got a little closer I noticed it was Billy Idol! Leee was really good at finding out about who was what, or who would let you do what. He had a real knack for seduction. I don't want to make him sound like a sleazy old oversexed queen—but he actually *is*.

John Waters: Punk rock music got me back into liking popular music. I didn't *like* any music between The Beatles and punk. I didn't listen to *any* music. I liked rhythm and blues so much that I thought The Beatles ruined rock 'n' roll. They were too sweet and nice. *Now* I like them; I'm not *against* them. But I didn't want to go to Woodstock—I wanted to go to Altamont. So when punk came along, it was so great—because we felt that we had *always* been punks, there just wasn't a word for it. When we made *Pink Flamingoes*, the colored hair—blue and red hair—you couldn't buy that in the drugstore. You had to strip your hair and use India ink or magic markers to dye your hair that color. Even though we made movies to shock hippies, in a way the point was—it was punk, we just didn't know it. So I was thrilled when it first came out. It got me back into popular music—to this day.

Eileen Myles: Punk culture was *art* culture. Punk, I feel, is a better name for postmodernity. And if there's any way to describe the art movement of my generation, it was *punk*—it was film, it was poetry, it was theater, it was music, it was everything.

Joanna Brown: I'm from Shreveport, Louisiana, and I ran away to Chicago when I was nineteen because it was the biggest city where I had a place to sleep when I got there. I got into punk rock when I was fifteen—I found the other three people in Shreveport who were into punk rock, and the one cool teacher and his wife that took us to see The Clash in Dallas, which was three hours away. And it changed my life forever. There was one store in Shreveport that sold non-top-40 records, they sold punk rock and weird shit. We'd meet on our bicycles and pedal over there to go through the stacks. And they sold a couple of offbeat magazines—*New York Rocker* and *Trouser Press*. One issue of the *New York Rocker* had a photo spread that was famous couples of punk rock. There was John Doe and Exene from X, and Les and Lene Lovich—and one of the couples was Adele Bertei and Lesley Woods from the Au Pairs. And I went off into a corner by myself and I was like, *Holy shit, there's* girls *in there, and they're a* couple, *and there's a picture of them and they're not ashamed!* And then there was an interview with Phranc, the Jewish lesbian folk singer, when her first record came out; and I realized—if you were a punk, that it was OK to be queer. It blew my mind!

2

GLORIOUSLY WRONG
THE LA SCENE (EARLY '80S)

Dennis Cooper: What's so interesting about the LA punk music scene was that it was very *queer*. You think about the major bands that were around; you had The Germs, and The Screamers, and The Bags, and Phranc, and Nervous Gender, and B People, and Human Hands—that were all queer, or at least partly queer. I was going to see all those shows and knew some of those people, and I was trying to combine things, trying to get everyone together and see what happened. And let poetry be a part of it—let poetry have some sort of adjunct . . . let poetry get some sort of shine off that whole thing.

Deke Nihilson: The LA scene was *crawling* with queer punks. Some of them more closeted, like Darby Crash, and some of them very out, like the Catholic Discipline people. And there were allies too, people who weren't queer—like, X was always right there. You see a lot of it in the London scene too—look at the Derek Jarman film *Jubilee*. Queers were always there as part of it. It wasn't like a queercore thing; it was just of *course*—it's where the freaks and the creatives and the misfits and the outcasts all came together and did their own thing. So of *course* there's going to be queers in it, and women, and a bunch of other people.

Don Bolles: We didn't need *queercore* back then because everything in Hollywood in some way *was* queercore. There was such a crazy diversity. Everyone that was part of the scene was either, like, a hustler on Hollywood Boulevard, like Bruce Barf, or Tony the Hustler, who was a good friend of ours—Darby lived with him for a while, he was a leather guy from Chicago . . . everyone did everything back then, except you weren't really supposed to like sex that much, you weren't supposed to obsess over it like the disco people. It wasn't like, *Hey, party, let's have sex!* That just looked gross to us. It was like, *Sex? Who cares? Let's jump around to crazy music. Fuck sex!*

I always say, when people ask, *Was Darby gay?* I go, *Well, y'know, that's a trick question.* Because gay people tended to like Barbra Streisand and Busby Berkeley

An early Germs leaflet from San Francisco

movies. Darby was *homosexual.* He liked to bone teenage skater boys and be boned by them.

Rik L. Rik was this gorgeous kid, he sang for this band called F-Word at the time, and he went around barefoot, and was really into, like, gothic kind of things. He was just gorgeous—Johnny Depp could have played him in a movie, except that he wasn't as cute as Rik L. Rick. Darby, I guess, got Rik to go back to his place with him. So one thing led to another, and at some point Darby was trying to seduce him, and he was telling him—*Hey, it's cool, y'know, the Greeks, the Romans . . .* Rik says that he didn't end up doing anything, but I don't know. I think it would have been very tough to say no to Darby, I mean everyone loved him. Even the people that hated everything he stood for wanted him to love them, to approve of them.

But he *was* worried that the way things were going with him and his sexuality, and with the hardcore punk scene coming to prominence, with Orange County jocks now being the main population at shows where at first they'd been a tiny minority—these people were not approving of homosexuality at *all.* But these were sort of the ranks of kids that Darby would choose his boyfriends from—he *liked* those Orange County skater kids, those Riverside skater kids. But he did not want anyone to know that he was gay.

Phranc: I grew up listening to folk music. The first rock and roll I listened to was Patti Smith. I didn't even—I was a complete folk music nerd growing up, and that's what I wanted to do. I dropped out of high school to be a lesbian. When I was seventeen I came out as a dyke, and I couldn't be a lesbian in my parents' house—so I left home, and spent most of my time in Venice, playing my guitar on the boardwalk for

SHOCK, SCREAMERS AND BACKSTAGE PASS AT STARWOOD 4TH OF JULY PARTY

What's this "party" business anyway? Where were the chips and guacamole dip? I'm very definite about what's a party and what's not. Lots of people are very definite about letting me in or not at THEIR party. But they wouldn't mind Shock crashing it, 'cause Shock are real nice and not shocking at all. The hostess would find them cute and well-behaved. It would be a nice evening unless The Screamers burst in, at which point the host would call the fire department and lock himself in the bathroom.

The Screamers are exponents of electrotherapy rock, and they even look it. You can almost smell the ether and hear the muffled gargles comin' from behind padded doors when they are onstage. Brain cells shrivel and eyeballs roll inward, forgotten muscles start twitching, foreign sounds come out of the throat. A definite departure from the routine. Even when they do slow songs like "Gloomy Sunday," the tension remains. There are slow songs and slow songs, and The Screamers do the latter kind. "Ziggy Stardust came out 5 years ago, and now it's SHIT! In five years, punk will be SHIT!" screams Tomato before the skull-crushing "Peer Pressure." Punks with a sense of history. Will these marvel-filled days never end? Will I ever sleep again?

All this commotion made it very hard for Backstage Pass to successfully carry the rest of the evening. Not mentioning the disturbing continuous barrage of firecrackers aimed at the performers. Why not frisbees, you anonymous peasants?

Kickboy

SLASH PAGE 25

Tomata du Plenty/The Screamers featured in *Slash*

money. Then I found out about this place called the Woman's Building, which was a feminist art institution in downtown Los Angeles. There were all these women, downtown, making art! I'd go there and I'd play my guitar in the bathroom, because the acoustics were really great, and that little community really embraced me.

Then I went up to San Francisco. I wanted to find some new lesbians, because of course San Francisco was the queer mecca. And instead of finding new lesbians, I found punk rock! I moved into a house on Howard Street, and The Avengers played our housewarming party . . . it was just kind of the beginning of my life. After being the outsider, being the queer kid in high school, not fitting in musically, not fitting in any way, I just thought I'd been born too late. I'd missed all the activism, everybody in school was apathetic . . . now suddenly I was with people who were my age, and they were really angry, and they were making art and music, and it was very exciting.

I had to come back to LA because I couldn't get a job in San Francisco. And I didn't know anyone in LA except for women from the Woman's Building, and some lesbians in the community here—but I was into *punk rock*, and the two worlds did not meet. All I wanted to do was be in a band, and find punk rock in LA. So I just started going to venues, by myself. I'd put on a little suit and tie and go out, and I'd stand against the wall and try to look cool. One night I was at Bases Hall on Vermont, and I was standing there in my suit and this guy came up to me and said, *Wanna be in a band?* And I was like, *Yeah!* They didn't ask me if I could play or sing or anything; I just *looked right*. And the band was Nervous Gender.

Don Bolles: They were really great. They played in new, artier spaces downtown like the Brave Dog, at First and Alameda. They were so good. I saw them in either late '78 or early '79, and I was blown away. It sounded like a swarm of insane bees, the synthesizers, and they were very dissonant. You could tell they weren't trying to be particularly dissonant; they were trying to play songs, but it was gloriously wrong. Frank was just banging on this Fender Jaguar completely out of tune, totally detuned actually. It was ridiculous, they were just the best. There were these three crazy synthesizer players, and this guitar player. They were even more flaming, they had a bigger flamer quotient than The Screamers.

Phranc: The music was so far from anything I would have made on my own. It was all electronic, keyboards, very angry—and kind of misogynist—queer music; but it was passionate, and I was *in a band*, with these three gay men. I wasn't in Nervous Gender for a long time; but we had a *good* time.

3

NOTHING WAS SACRED
VAGINAL DAVIS IN LA

Brontez Purnell: Raquel Gutiérrez, who's a poet, once told me that Vaginal Creme Davis's influence was totally ubiquitous to LA.

Kathleen Hanna: Vaginal Creme Davis? She is a wonderful performer, singer, scene-maker, scene-stealer, *shrimper*—I don't know how to describe her, writer? Queercore legend.

Sarah Schulman: Vaginal Davis— she was one of the, the actual, very first queercore person.

Vaginal Davis: I attracted a lot of attention at that time in the late 1970s. All the kids that looked weird got a lot of attention. I didn't think of myself as looking so weird at the time. I pretty much looked similar to the way I look now. Always had my hair very short or shaved, and my standard look was very thin, straight-leg pants. I kinda look the way like people looked in the early 1960s. That was sort of like

Vaginal Davis and Joan Jett Blakk at SPEW 2. Photo by Mark Freitas

my little uniform. Well, when I wasn't all dolled up, when I wasn't like wearing, y'know . . . I went between my casual sort of early 1960s look and then my fancier look was doing sort of silent movie-star drag.

Jürgen Brüning: Vaginal is two meters tall, and I'm only 1.68 meters, so I always have to look up whenever I talk to her. She is this amazing person who loves to talk. I've had the chance to meet and work with Vaginal several times over the years. I'm not sure when I met her though. Maybe on the shoot for Bruce LaBruce's *Hustler White* in Los Angeles? I'm not sure. But she lives in Berlin now and does theater projects with [frequent Bruce LaBruce star] Susanne Sachße. It's great.

Vaginal Davis: When I first started, it was the late 1970s and I was putting together urban Blaxploitation looks and commentary and original music. I was writing these weird sort of songs—I didn't think they were punk songs at all. I thought they were more like showtunes. Because of my lack of skill; it came off more as punk rock than showtunes. But I was using as my examples Hollywood musicals. Everyone thought that I was so weird, because it hadn't become retro yet. I wasn't born middle class and I didn't ever feel like I was fully integrated into full punk scene. When I started to actually perform doing my own thing with my first group, The Afro Sisters, I felt like a lot of the punks didn't know where to put The Afro Sisters.

Bruce LaBruce: When we were doing *J.D.s* in Toronto we thought we were the only ones who had this kind of . . . philosophy. Then we started reaching out, making fanzines, and finding people in other cities. And it turned out Vaginal was making work in Los Angeles that was very simpatico. She had her fanzine, *Fertile La Toyah Jackson*, and I thought she was the most glamorous woman I had ever encountered. We used to write long rambling letters to each other. So we were very connected even before we met. And when I

Fertile La Toyah Jackson Magazine

went down to LA to show *No Skin off My Ass* there for the first time, I stayed with her, in her crummy little apartment on Sunset Boulevard. And I thought it was extremely glamorous.

Vaginal Davis: At the time, there were only a few queercore/homocore magazines. And one of the earliest ones was my magazine: *Fertile La Toyah Jackson*. It lasted for about ten years, but I only had about six issues. One issue lasted for so long because I never dated them and never wrote about things that could date them. And as long as I was getting orders, I kept printing new copies. I think that's one of the differences between a magazine like mine and *Flipside* or *Maximum Rocknroll*—they were dated. I called them "The Visual Issue" or "The Harvest Issue" or "The Paris Issue," you know? I would never like say "FLT Volume One, July 3, 1983." And I did that on purpose, because I just wanted it to like last for a long time. It still looks like nothing else out there.

Kembra Pfahler: I met Vaginal Davis in Los Angeles in the early '90s. She was hosting an event—a club. This was at a time when Ron Athey and Rick Owens and a lot of other artists that I really admire were all living in Los Angeles. I can remember growing up in Los Angeles always feeling extremely devalued; I felt like people were very sizeist, and misogynist, and sexist toward me or whatever, so much so that I created this incredibly large persona in Karen Black to excavate all of that shame that I had embedded in me for so many years. And I remember meeting Ms. Davis. At the time I was a much younger artist, and Ms. Davis really took me seriously, and I instantly felt this incredible respect—mutual respect—about the work that we were both doing. At that time, people really didn't take seriously a five-foot-one, hundred-pound punk rock girl. I mostly was derided, y'know; my look wasn't popular at the time, I hadn't been discovered by Calvin Klein, people threw things at me when I walked down the street, and they would yell *Scary Sherri!* or *Vampira!* or whatever. So I had this instant connection with Ms. Davis. And I think she's a very important part of this generation of queer artists, someone that married different genders, different sexual backgrounds. Homosexuality was no longer exclusive and separatist. I think that's something that Bruce and Ms. Davis are really responsible for. And Ron Athey, too. The circle of people that they engaged with was inclusive; it wasn't separatist, it wasn't misogynist. I think it was really a turning point for queer culture. And Ms. Davis taking me under her wing, y'know—*come with me*. I'm just so grateful to her for that. Besides the fact that she's an incredible linguist, an incredible visual artist, an incredible lyricist, and . . . presence. She's a great beauty.

Vaginal Davis: Dennis Cooper was a contributing editor at *Artforum* and had written about my Hag Gallery and then he wrote about the zines. He was the one who said: "Vaginal Davis is the future of art." He wrote this grandiose tag . . . that I was the future of art. At that time, I didn't know what *Artforum* was. I had no idea what it was. I was written up in all these like highbrow art magazines like *Art in America*, *Artforum*. I didn't know even about these magazines. This shows how naive I was, because I was really young then.

Genesis P-Orridge: I encountered Bruce LaBruce in Los Angeles, through Glen Meadmore who is in *Hustler White*. Glen is immensely tall and used to work as a duo with Vaginal Davis. They did a really aggressive cabaret act together. They both are over six-foot-six; they would wear sort of Cockette punk. Because they were so big and strong, they would literally grab somebody in the front row, who they assumed was straight, drag him on stage, attack him with dead chickens, and stick their asses on his face—overwhelm him in a quite brutally aggressive way. And they always picked the one who looked the most normal and butch to humiliate.

Billy Miller: Yeah, Vag is hilarious, Vag is just a funny person all the way around. And the kind of humour that I can relate to. A title like *Fertile La Toyah Jackson* is just funny. And she had some great shows—Cholita and some other groups.

Vaginal Davis: Cholita were the Female Menudo, my band with Alice Bag. When we worked on Cholita in the 1980s, it came in a period where I was very much not interested in any kind of alternative music culture things. I stopped like listening to punk rock or anything rock 'n' roll oriented or anything underground. It would appear that I kind of divorced myself from the whole scene and I was only listening to Spanish-language music, especially this radio station called K-Radio Amore: K-LOVE. And it was playing Mexican pop music or Spanish pop music. The Afro Sisters sort of like went idle. Or we stopped really performing and then Cholita emerged. Cholita! emerged as sort of like Latina all-girl-pop group who were all teenagers between the ages of twelve and fourteen. And the minute you turn fifteen, you're too old and you get kicked out, like Menudo, the Puerto Rican boy group. One time we performed on this big street scene in Silver Lake called The Sunset Junction. It's a big, big festival that they had every year in Silver Lake. And we performed on the main stage there and some women from a TV show completely believed our backstory from the group, that we were all teenagers—even though at that time it was the mid-1990s, like '94 or something. So I was maybe thirty-two. This woman from a television show, she says "Oh, I would like you guys to be on this TV show. Perform on the show but then also bring your mothers." As big as I am, she thought I was under fifteen, y'know. If you do anything really convincing enough on stage, people believe it. And then, I remember she was talking to us and staying still in character, I said, *Oh, you want us?* And it was like one of these talk shows. And we said, *Oh, you want us to be on that talk show? Isn't that a little exploitative?* And she said, *Oh no, because there will be a psychologist on the show too.*

Tony Arena: Her performances are like nothing that I've ever seen. Brilliant, y'know. Brilliant performances. Eventually I got so happy that I got to be in a G.B. Jones movie with Vaginal Davis, *The Lollipop Generation* . . . an awesome movie.

Scott Treleaven: Humor was one of the things that made queercore so amazing. Whenever things got a little too straight-faced, someone was there to interject some—sometimes wonderfully vicious—humor into things. Vaginal Davis was like a saint—she was able to send up anything. Nothing was sacred—still isn't. She's kind of perfection in that way.

4

FACTION
TORONTO'S "FABRICATED" SCENE
(MID-1980S–EARLY 1990S)

A young G.B. Jones and Bruce LaBruce

G.B. Jones: I had been in a band called Bunny & the Lakers, with Peter Morgan, Howard Pope and Wendy King. And we had broken up amicably when Peter moved to England and Howard moved to New York. They'd been good friends, so I was really depressed. I told my friend John Brown, the painter, and he suggested that I go meet these two girls, Janet and Kathleen, who were starting a band. So I went over to their house, and I told them I could play drums, even though I'd never played drums before.

    We were just starting out, so we were hanging around with our friends rather than trying to be part of a scene. And really, our *own* scene evolved out of that, playing with bands like Rongwrong, The Woods Are Full of Cuckoos, The Party's Over. It was a very separate scene from anything going on in Toronto at the time. I think all of our bands were what would later be called post-punk, rather than being first-generation punk; we were more experimental, weirder. People would call us "art-damaged."

The first zine I ever worked on was called *Hide*. It was a zine that my friend Candy and Caroline Azar had started, and they asked me to help with it. They were doing really exciting things; Caroline was doing amazing work with xerox, just taking every object she could find—pieces of lath, chain-link fence—she was xeroxing it all, creating the most amazing collages out of these objects that I'd never have thought of xeroxing. I'd had an instructor in college, Barbara Astman, who'd introduced me to

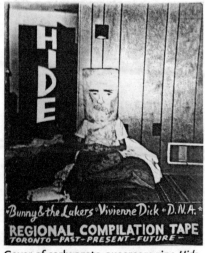

Cover of early proto-queercore zine *Hide*

xerox art and xerox photography, and I was just in love with xerox machines, I thought they were the best thing in the world.

Caroline had come up the idea that she wanted to have not just a paper zine but also include a cassette with each issue. We were really interested in the whole cassette culture that was going on in the 1980s. We had stuff in *Hide* that was queer-related—people don't really know that, but *Hide* was kind of like the gateway to *J.D.s*. Someone doing a whole article about hustlers they had met, for instance.

Bruce LaBruce: Just Desserts was the ground zero where I met a lot of people involved with the queercore movement in Toronto. It was a kind of bourgeois dessert restaurant, run by this ex-hippie art student who hired all these freaks and misfits to torture and terrorize the clientele; that's what people went to the restaurant for, basically. I was a film student at York University, and there were eight or nine of us working during the day shift—all film students at York University. And then these punks, junkies and musicians were all working the night shift. That's where I met G.B. Jones.

Mark Freitas and G.B. Jones in G.B.'s apartment, ca. 1989 or 1990.

I was already experimenting a lot with style; I've always had my hair bleached or shaved—I was looking a bit *Liquid Sky* in those days, and she had her big red fright wig, and her tights, and her motorcycle boots. It was partly style, really, to begin with. And then politics. I was studying film theory and social and political thought in university; my professor, Robin Wood, was a hardcore Marxist feminist. So I was getting my political education in the university, and then I was getting my punk education at work, at Just Desserts. We had these long shifts—it was an all-night restaurant, open until three a.m. on weekdays and twenty-four hours on weekends. So we had a lot of time to sit around, to learn, to talk and plan and scheme and create revolutions in our coffee cups.

I met Fifth Column while working at the restaurant, and started go-go dancing for them shortly after that—a kind of feminist gesture, reversing the objectification of the body, and the gender—so instead of the usual kind of decorative female go-go dancing it was a girl band with a male go-go dancer.

Then I moved in with them, with Fifth Column. We lived in this ramshackle, squat-like building in east Toronto, at Queen and Parliament. The building was really falling apart and decrepit. There was a double storefront: the Fifth Column rehearsal space was in one storefront and my bedroom was in the other. There was no heat downstairs, so I was always upstairs, where G.B. lived; we'd sit upstairs where it was warm and do our zine *J.D.s*, cutting and pasting and writing our manifestos.

G.B. Jones: If one was to look for the genesis of *J.D.s*, it really starts with Caroline Azar. Most people have never given her any credit for this, but . . . in the early '80s she started working at what people

Cover of Fifth Column's *All Time Queen of the World*

would call a dive bar, called Together's. Caroline's background is in theater, and so her incredible ability to assemble a *cast* around her came into play. We met Joe the Ho there, this hustler who would wear these amazing, cute little mod shirts and this short little haircut—hustlers just didn't look like that, then. And all sorts of weird punk kids and older dykes . . . it was an economically diverse bar, where people from different strata of society would socialize—people that were poor, people that were working-class, punks, hustlers.

Then she started putting on shows there. She would have, like, an experimental film night, where she'd get filmmakers like John Porter, I had one of my films show there . . . and people were extremely receptive. Then Caroline got me a job as a DJ there. I'd play what I called punk lite—Siouxsie and the Banshees, Blondie, just stuff I thought people would like. And the bar ended up becoming enormously popular. Then Caroline arranged a night where Fifth Column would play; so then we had live music coming into the situation. I was really fascinated by the phenomenon of what was happening there.

I had been going to a used bookstore, and I'd found these really old tabloids that had been published in Toronto, called things like *Tattler* and *Midnight*. They'd have columns in them written by gay people, reports on what was happening in the gay scene, like, such-and-such hustler did this thing this week . . . and I thought, wow, this is incredible! It was like a gossip column, all about people at the St. Charles, and the Blue Jay. I thought it would be really exciting to start a zine that did the same

fifth column / & bruce labruce

photo: Jacquie

Sitting in his den,
the principal feels lonely,
wants a tomboy,tom-boy,Tom Boy.
His wife does wonder
if there's a plan. (?)
Looking so lovingly to her man.
Holding his heart in her hands.

Sitting in her wheelchair,
raven hair now's got grey.
Raven hair now's got grey.
"Hey, where are my car keys,
I'm going to the mall,honey."

- (Gossip)
Caroline: He took the family car
            to Fairview Mall...
Bruce LaB: Get her!
C: He went to Kresges, then
   went down the hall...
B: Mary don't prance!
C: Went to the washroom and
   hid in a stall...
B: What's a boy to do?
C: Met a young man and took a fall.
B: Hmmm...(heavy sigh)
C: Then, staring at each other,
   they answered the call.
B: Pay it no mind, girl.

CHORUS

- (more gossip)
Caroline: And so the saga continues...
Bruce LaB: Boys just want to have fun!
C: The young man gave the older man a
   blowjob and he, uh, took it all.
B: Yummy yummy yummy I got love in my
   tummy!
C: Then the cops burst in, to protect
   the mall.
B: Don't rain on my parade!
C: Do you think this country has
   a lot of gall?
B: Uh-Huh!
C: PUT IT TO MUSIC GIRL!

The Fairview Mall Story.

AS RECORDED BY FIFTH COLUMN
ON "TO SIR WITH HATE" L.P.
AVAILABLE ON HIDE RECORDS

Lyric sheet to Fifth Column's "The Fairview Mall Story"

thing for our crowd at Together's. So I asked Bruce if he wanted to make
a zine with me, and we started *J.D.s*.

The pictures of Bruce and Joe the Ho that were in the first issue I
took at Together's—most of the people in the first issue were people
that went to Together's and hung out with Caroline. Anita from Fifth
Column, her sister Angela, and their friends—and they were hardcore
punks, so these hardcore punk girls would come in with their huge
mohawks, and all the old dykes would go, *Oh, your hair is so pretty!* It was
just the most incredible scene. And I was taking pictures of everyone
there and putting them in *J.D.s*; and that's basically how it started.

At the same time, Caroline had the idea to do this song called "The Fairview Mall Story," which was about the bust, at the Fairview Mall, of these men who'd been having sex in the washroom, and the police surveillance that caught them. The police then released the list of their names to the radio, and the radio announcers read their names over the air and their lives were horribly ruined, and one of them committed suicide, so Caroline wanted to write a song about that. And not too many people were doing stuff like that.

Bruce LaBruce: "The Fairview Mall Story" was the song that I performed with Fifth Column most often. It was based on a true-life incident that happened around that time, these married men getting busted for having gay sex in the public bathrooms of a shopping mall. I had a little rap with Caroline in the middle of the song and then I would go-go dance.

G.B. Jones: That song inspired me to look among all the hardcore records that Candy had—because it seemed like there *were* some other groups that had weird songs about gay stuff. Mighty Sphincter had a song called "Gay Bar," the Leather Nun had a song—I think it was a cover of the ABBA song "I Need a Man," something like that—and I think the Leather Nuns probably *were* queer. Some people were doing it as a joke; some people were letting their sexuality creep in; it was all very ambiguous, which I thought was really interesting.

Bruce LaBruce: *J.D.s* was really music-based, so we had a list, a homocore list of top-ten bands that we really liked, that had gay-themed songs—everyone from Patti Smith to the Ramones to underground punk bands like Aryan Disgrace. The Nip Drivers was one of our favorites, who had a song about Quentin Crisp. And I loved The Ugly Americans, who were a straight punk band who had a song against homophobia. And then we had bands that actually started forming and contributing original music to *J.D.s*.

G.B. Jones: I had no problem putting in a band with a homophobic song and claiming that this was all part of the new queercore movement. What better way to get revenge on them than to claim that they're part of a movement of queers in punk music? So Bruce and I kind of put across the idea that this was a huge international movement. And people believed it! That was the shocking part. We'd have all these songs, we'd write up these lists, and people just thought, *Oh, this is really happening!* And lo and behold, the next thing we knew there *were* all these bands, sending us songs so we could put out our own cassette compilations. And from there it just took off.

J.D.s "Homocore Top Ten"

Bruce LaBruce: We were influenced by the Situationists—so we had this idea of *spectacle*, creating a kind of spectacle that was, in a way, a parody of pop culture and in a parallel way, like Warhol's superstars, a parody of Hollywood, yet they *became* real superstars. So we created an illusion that there was a full-fledged queer punk movement happening in Toronto, dykes and faggots and transgender people, to the extent that people—like Gus Van Sant says, he came to Toronto to make *To Die For* and was expecting to find this crazy queer punk scene that was thriving and ubiquitous, and it was just me and three dykes, basically.

Dennis Cooper: I mean, I visited Johnny and Rex a couple of times, and G.B., and that's exactly what was going on—there was *nothing* going on. It was all happening in their houses. I mean, a little later it picked up because Scott Treleaven started doing his stuff. But at that time, it was all just a big fantasy, right? It was a fantasy, what was happening in Toronto.

Mark Freitas: The way they made it sound, in *J.D.s*, it really took on these epic proportions—it was like when I was a midwestern boy living in rural Michigan and I would subscribe to *Details* and *Interview* and the *Village Voice* and imagine New York—oh my god, this amazing scene!—I had the same kind of gigantic picture of this scene in Toronto.

Tony Arena: It didn't sound fake when I was reading *J.D.s*. I know they always say, *We were writing about a scene that didn't in fact exist.* I was like—*I* think it exists. Even if it's just four or five people, that's a scene and those people do exist. Fifth Column did exist as a band. A few people can be a scene. A few people is more than me, one kid alone in my bedroom drawing pictures of gay guys. To me, writing to those people in Toronto, they had a scene that they were making, and even if it was just a few people it was more than just me alone. And then suddenly it exploded into this huge global thing—and thank god it did. But when I was alone, that was a big deal—that there were a handful of queer punks hanging out together, having parties. That was a big deal to me.

Glenn Belverio: When you start to fabricate something, it's like—Diana Vreeland, one of my muses, my icons. Mrs. Vreeland called it *faction*, a combination of fact and fiction. In the case of homocore they needed to do it because there weren't very many gay people who wanted to listen to punk rock—they were listening to whatever, very bad dance music. So they had to make it seem like it was a bigger movement than it really was. Of course, it *became* a real movement. Through the distribution of zines and tapes it grew into a global phenomenon.

Kathleen Hanna: We didn't really know how big the scene in Toronto was, with *J.D.s* and G.B., but I did know that G.B. was multifaceted— she was making films, she was making zines, she was in a band. And I had the same sort of drive. I'm the kind of person who is constantly making shit. I was born to make shit, so I really related to her on that level, trying to create a scene. Later on, when I did one of the only mainstream-press interviews I did, for the *LA Weekly*, and I was asked about riot grrrl—we'd had just two meetings, in Washington, DC, but I was like, *Riot grrrl is all over the country; there are meetings happening everywhere—Minneapolis, Chicago, LA*—I just made up a bunch of places and I was like, *Yeah, there are meetings all over, we started this thing, and it's totally a phenomenon.* And then it *became* a phenomenon, because I said it was. That article came out and then girls started looking for the meetings. And I remember having the feeling that that's was what the girls in Toronto were doing. They were, like, five people but they made it seem like it was so huge. I liked that they felt like they could do that— that they were such bitches, that they thought they just could take over everything. And more than anything that influenced me—that they were bitches. They were bitches with style.

G.B. Jones: We really started in the anarchist community. We didn't really start in the gay community. We were trading with anarchist zines and meeting anarchists from the States, and that was really our milieu—the punk scene, the post-punk scene, experimental filmmakers and artists. So we met all these people when we were touring and we'd show our films, and that's how it started spreading. We'd take the zines with us when we traveled; we were kind of like this traveling circus, y'know—*here's the band!*, and *here's the zine!*, and *here's the movies!* It was very much like the Exploding Plastic Inevitable. And I think that's how it spread so quickly, because people were encountering it so many different levels.

Tom Jennings: In San Francisco we were creating this mythology of queer punk that did not exist. That was the point. It really did not exist. People started reading *Homocore*, and, I think, perceiving that there was a queer punk subculture in San Francisco when it was really just Deke and me. Whether we were doing this intentionally or not, I don't really remember. But there was a lot of spontaneous . . . almost nothing gets invented by one person alone. Almost all inventions are responses to human culture. So while Deke and I were doing *Homocore*, the people in Toronto had been doing their thing. There's a moment of simulta- neous discovery. If you invent something and no one's ever heard of it, it remains obscure because no one knows what to do with it. So Homocore had to make sense in some context. And with all the other zines it did. They were all contemporary responses to the pressures of the time.

Jon Ginoli: Before the Sex Pistols formed, Malcolm McLaren had this idea of what he wanted a band to be like—*before* there was a band like that, *before* there was a scene. It's kind of the same with homocore, with G.B. Jones and Bruce LaBruce in Toronto dreaming up this scene when there wasn't any. But culturally it was a ripe idea.

Bruce LaBruce: When you make a fiction, when you create an idealistic world with these fanzines, it's like a fantasy of how you want to be per- ceived by the world. So for me personally, I created Bruce LaBruce—this hard, punk character that was militant and aggressive, but also making porn, and creating havoc, breaking the law, shoplifting, getting his lips sewn shut, which I did several times. So it was a creation of a persona, but it was also a fiction, a performance.

And of course, all the other people who were doing fanzines—I realized they were doing the same thing. So in LA, Vaginal Davis was creating this kind of glamazon character . . . My idea of that whole scene in LA was similar to other people's idea of what was going on in Toronto with *J.D.s*—I mean, she created this whole glamorous fantasy world. And when I got there—with her, it kind of *did* live up to the expectations, but it was much smaller, more down and dirty. She lived in a crummy little apartment and had a day job at UCLA. So it's more grounded in reality when you meet people in real life.

5

CAUGHT IN THE CRACKS
BETWEEN *GAY* AND *PUNK*

Adam Rathe: Queercore wasn't just against homophobia and the martyring of gay people. It was against the mainstream gay society, against the idea of upper-class white men going to the gym and spending their nights at the baths. It was against dance music, it was against small dogs and summer houses.

Bruce LaBruce: For us the gay scene was completely bourgeois and conventional, and we didn't feel welcome in that scene either. In fact, in Toronto there was a gay bar in the gay ghetto that we sort of adopted as our unofficial headquarters, and we used to hang out there all the time because we *wanted* to participate in the gay world. But we didn't really feel welcome in the gay bars. I mean, I would get kicked out of the gay bars in Toronto for wearing swastika earrings. I wasn't welcome. My style wasn't welcome. I couldn't get laid—except in a bathhouse, when I had all my clothes off.

Part of my position has always been that I was rejected by two subcultures, the gay subculture and the punk subculture. I've never really felt like I've fit into either of them. So I've always felt like I'm on the fringe of the fringe. Like even the fringe elements—my work is either too extreme for them or doesn't fit into the kind of orthodoxy that these subcultures have. It's the same with my work in art versus pornography: the art world quite often views my work as too pornographic, and the porn people think that my work is too arty, so I'm caught in the cracks somewhere between the two. So that's always informed my work and my identity, this idea of either being too extreme for the extreme edge of a subculture or just not fitting in anywhere—being a total misfit.

DON'T BE GAY, OR,
HOW I LEARNED TO STOP WORRYING AND FUCK PUNK UP THE ASS

by G.B. Jones (dyke division) and Bruce LaBruce (fag division)
for the New Lavender Panthers

[This article appeared in MAXIMUMROCKNROLL Feb. 89, for the sexuality issue (the best ever MRR issue). The response was... underwhelming. It ain't a problem with the article. You figure it out. Reprinted without permission. – tj]

HAS PUNK FAILED?

As part of our preparation for this article, and included in the latest issue of JD's [#4? #3? – tj], our homocore fanzine, we devised a questionnaire on the subject of gays and punks. Question number six implored you to go to the dictionary and look up "punk" too see if you'd feel any different afterwards.

    Q. Go to the dictionary. Look up "punk". Did you do it? Honest? Did you feel any different?

    A. No, I don't feel any different, just smarter
        – Jane Guskin / YEASTIE GIRLZ

        I don't own a dictionary
        – Gerard " Conflict" Cosloy

        What was the purpose of that?
        – Marc Rentzer / LETCH PATROL

        No, I didn't do it, because I don't have a dictionary "handy"
        – anonymous wimp

If you weren't too busy, and you managed to find it, here's the definition of punk that might have confronted you:

    punk (pungk) slang noun 1 An inexperienced or callow youth 2 A young tough 3 A passive homosexual, or catamite

(If you *really* did your homework, you would've discovered that punk is also an archaic word for dried wood used for tinder, the original meaning of the word "faggot" as well. Homosexuals, witches, criminals, all denounced as enemies of the state, were once burned at the stake. The word for the material used to set them on fire became another name for the victims themselves. It's no accident that "punk" and "faggot" have a similar root.)

Whaddyaknow. Punks are fags, too. Better start worrying now. Long before 'punk' meant mohawks and MAXIMUMROCKNROLL, young boys were being 'turned out' in jail (recruited to serve other prisoners' sexual desires) and labeled 'punks' ("I punked the kid"). Displaying homemade tattoos and a distaste for authority, these original punks, many of them delinquent minors imprisoned for breaking society's rules, became, on the inside, *sexual* outlaws as well. This was *the* point of identification for the early 'punk rockers' who emerged in the mid-seventies, explicitly playing out the role of 'the punk' in dress, attitude, and the rejection of social norms. This stance *obviously* included sexual delinquency – looking for *bad* trouble by, for example, acting like 42nd Street hustlers (Dee Dee Ramone, Patti Smith, among others, in the U.S.) or wearing a t-shirt with two guys fucking on it (Sid and Johnny in the U.K.).

    Q. Has anybody ever called you a fag or dyke because you are a punk?

    A. Yes! Yeastie Girls get called dykes all the time.
        – Jane Guskin

        Yes, but because I was a real punk
        – anonymous wimp

        Yeah, and then she asked me for some lipstick.
        – Jim

        Yes
        – Lawrence Livermore / LOOKOUT

The phenomenon of a highly visible and disruptive subculture looking sexually deviant and seeming to behave that way has proven an effective weapon against institutions that attempt to control and contain personal identity and sexual freedom. So what does it mean when someone calls you a fag or dyke? Society considers you as outside of its restraints and controls, and that your protest must extend to sexual behavior as well. The next time someone calls you queer, consider the implications. Maybe you've got them right where you want them.

Early punks, and, judging from our questionnaire, some punks still today, fuck around with people's conservative notions about sex roles. But as a 'movement', it doesn't seem like punk has clued in to the idea of using sex as a strategy for promoting change. So the obvious question *we're* asking is:

What is the Failure of Punk?

Let's face it. Going to most punk shows today is lot like going to the average fag bar (MIGHTY SPHINCTER notwithstanding): all you see is big macho 'dudes' in leather jackets and jeans parading around the dance floor/pit, manhandling each other's sweaty bodies in proud display. The only difference is that at the fag bar, females have been almost completely banished, while at the punk club, they've just been relegated to the periphery, but allowed a pretense of participation (ie. girlfriend, groupie, go-fer, or post-show pussy). In this highly masculinized world, the focus is doubly male, the boys on stage controlling the 'meaning' of the event (the style of music, political message, etc), and the boys in the pit determining the extent of the exchange between audience and performer. And where does this leave the rest? 'Wimpy' boys, with glasses, maybe, who can't compete, or girls who aren't exactly encouraged to participate? Unless, of course, they're willing to take a stand against 'all that macho crap'. (There are of course exceptions to the male rule: girl bands or bands that include women as equal participants, or bands like the CRUCIFUCKS and the RYTHYM PIGS who pointedly criticize macho behavior during shows.)

The gay 'movement' as it exists now is a big farce, and we have nothing else to say about it, so we won't say anything

2¬7

An excerpt from G.B. Jones and Bruce LaBruce's "Don't Be Gay, or, How I Learned to Stop Worrying and Fuck Punk up the Ass" manifesto originally printed in *Maximum Rocknroll*

Andrew Martini: I think everyone in Limp Wrist who is gay has had a sort of dressed-down stage, trying to fit into a more mainstream gay scene. When I was about twenty-five I started going to gay bars. This was around when Limp Wrist started. I started going to gay bars and trying to fit in with people there, but I didn't really connect with people because it was more like a pop culture kind of thing, and I wasn't really into that at the time. But everyone in Limp Wrist to a certain degree has tried to do that, and then come back and been like, *Yeah . . . I don't really need to be accepted in that scene—it's cool.*

Martín Sorrondeguy: Growing up a Catholic boy, going to Catholic school all the way through high school, being an altar boy, being a Cub Scout, Boy Scout—anything that really went against all that really appealed to me. I was always searching for something weird and different. Punk came into my world starting with cousins that we visited in New York. As a kid I always liked Kiss, because they were weird and they wore makeup. Then in 1979 my family went to New York and my cousins had, like, Ramones ticket stubs up on their wall. And ever since that stuff entered my world, I was fascinated by it. In terms of my queerness, my gayness, that was so much riskier to dive into, and I came out way later. There was the punk rock, for a long time, and I just ignored sex for a long time.

I was straddling two worlds. Before I got heavily into punk, there was this underground house scene, these dance crews that were made up of mostly Latino and black kids. The Culitos were one of the most popular crews, they would do these amazing house dancing routines, and they were openly, out queer kids in the hood. Talk about risky—I mean, these kids were putting it out there. I remember this one kid had a curly mohawk, dyed blonde, and glittery makeup—this is broad daylight—at Division and Western, in 1983. People were freaking out . . . but there was this wave of queerness that went through all the neighborhoods tied to house music. So when I was going to punk shows at the Metro, and it was really *tough*—there were a lot of skinheads in Chicago, a lot of craziness—I found my way to navigate those two worlds. Like, *I'm gonna go here to get my punk, but I know where to go to get my dick.*

Then the time came when I couldn't ignore it anymore, I kind of knew where I had to go. It ended up happening where I went on a tour with Los Crudos, and I realized that I couldn't fight these feelings I was having anymore. I did it in this weird way where I came out in Chicago last. I came out in all these different cities. It was like a drive-by come-out. And it was going really well. Then, finally, it was at the Fireside Bowl one night, and I just said it. I was at home, y'know, and it's hard to come out at home. And it was awesome—so many kids just rushed the stage and stood up for me.

Scott Treleaven: I realized fairly early on with regards to sexuality—it's a component of our personalities that's hardwired to a bunch of other things, that influences behavior and worldview in some really fundamental ways. It wasn't simply about who I was fucking; it was much deeper. And when you realize that you're queer and you look back at the way that you've been treated, the way you're supposed to think about yourself in relationship to society—you're perverse or you're evil, any of these pejorative terms that have been thrown at you—when you realize that's fundamentally wrong, and that you know *innately* that you're connecting with something that's not only correct but natural, there's a process that you go through where you start to analyze all the other systems you're involved in. *What else have I been told that's not true? What else have I been convinced of that's actually false? What else is supported and sustained by society that may be artificial?* So I think the alignment of queer and punk was really natural. Punk has always questioned the status quo, and of course queers should too.

Jody Bleyle: Let's say you're a punk, you're starting to grow up, you're getting older, and you see the adult world in front of you and just think, *That's not my world. I don't see a place for myself there.* And when you're queer you look ahead of you and you don't see a place for yourself there either. So in that sense there's a real commonality. I think there was a real desperation—I mean, it felt like life or death to me. I felt like if I didn't find some dykes to play music with—not just any music but the music that was, like, my sole connection to the universe—I couldn't imagine living, I couldn't imagine actually going on. I couldn't imagine how I would be able to do that, so it felt like life or death.

Brontez Purnell: I think I was fifteen, sixteen, seventeen, y'know the years get blurry, but I was in Alabama and my drama teacher called gay people a genetic mistake. So I wrote a letter to Kathleen Hanna and told her, and she wrote me back. She gave me the first Le Tigre CD and she was like—I still have the letter somewhere—"Don't worry about it, you shouldn't feel pressure about your sexuality or whatever." And it was a couple years later when I was eighteen and I moved to Bloomington and

I went on tour with Le Tigre and Panty Raid. And she remembered me because she said she kept my picture as a bookmark for years.

Deke Nihilson: By the middle-to-late '80s, hardcore punk rock for a lot of people was an alternative way to be meathead. And meanwhile, by that point, AIDS had already devastated the gay community, and you started seeing this shift, historically, from the Gay Liberation Front-era demands for life on our own terms to—of necessity—pleading with the state for resources, for research, for people who were dying. Out of that came this sort of assimilationist thrust, demanding the right to get married and have kids in the suburbs like everybody else—*We're just like anybody else except for who we're sleeping with!*—which we didn't feel was in the spirit of the early gay rights movements. In a wider cultural sense, this assimilationism was always something that punk rock actively critiqued, so we kind of felt that we were putting the punk back in the homo movement and the homo back in the punk movement at the same time.

Jena von Brucker: I think we felt ostracized by gay culture. There were a lot things going on in that culture that we didn't like. There was lot of separation between men and women, there was a lot of hostility toward women. So there was a certain amount of anger that fueled the things that we said about the gay establishment. Some of what we said was harsh, but I think we were calling attention to things that needed attention. Could it have been said in a different way? Yes—there were probably people who said it in a really nice way, in an academic way. We said it in a very confrontational way. But it's not that those things didn't have to be said.

Bruce LaBruce: We were against all sorts of orthodoxies, G.B. Jones and I. We didn't call ourselves artists; we thought the art world was corrupt at that point. We thought that the gay orthodoxy was bullshit and bourgeois. But then any sort of "legitimate" queer activism we were very suspicious of; we were also very suspicious of the anarchist movement—because I've never seen a more bureaucratic institution than the anarchist movement. It was impossible to get anything done, everything had to be done by committee and everything was talked to death. In terms of activism it wasn't nimble enough, it was entrenched in all sorts of dogma. So we always skipped around that kind of stuff and always considered ourselves outsiders among the outsiders.

Brontez Purnell: How the hell are two tech workers with an exponentially greater amount of wealth, living with their boyfriends, how are me and them the same people necessarily? I feel like the straight men that I've lived with in my life over the years, I feel like they're more my people than those other people. Just because we like to suck dick and fuck booty-hole, we're all the same person? That can't be right. That can't be real.

Mykel Board: In the '70s, the hets wanted to be like the homos. The hets looked at the homos and said, *Man, they have sex all over the place, they're free, they don't get tied down.* So they started these swingers clubs, trying to imitate the homo lifestyle. They wanted all the fun that the homos were having at that time. When Plato's Retreat opened, it was an imitation of a gay sex club—it happened to be guys and girls together, but otherwise it was just a gay sex club. That was considered wild and exciting.

Now it's completely reversed. Gay people want to imitate the het lifestyle. They want to get married, they want to adopt children, they want to fit in society. There's *going* to be a gay president. And . . . it's really sad, the changes that have happened. I think it's really awful to be gay now. When I hear somebody say *I'm queer* or *I'm homo*—yeah! But *I'm gay* is so respectable, it gives me the creeps. Respectable people generally give me the creeps; but people who naturally have a way out of this cage of respectability and they don't take it, they just want to get inside and shut the door, those people really give me the creeps.

Bruce Benderson: What disturbs me about the word *punk* is that it *used* to have such a strong political signification. It was an expression of working-class frustration. Now, say you're from a lawyer's family, like me; you grow up in the best part of town and start hanging out at punk concerts but are otherwise apolitical, what exactly are you expressing? I don't know; maybe you're vicariously getting off on that working-class energy, in the same way that the bohemians who came to poor neighborhoods vicariously got off on the energy of the lumpenproletariat and created art. I believe that every single avant-garde was created out of that experience. And the reason we don't have a vibrant avant-garde *now* is because that essential link between bohemia and the culture of poverty that led to every single avant-garde—Baudelaire, the flâneur, walking through the worst neighborhoods at night, taking a bath of degeneration and being inspired by that; Norman Mailer calling himself a "white negro"; and so on—no longer exists.

It was *my* generation who started to *ruin* that equation. And I think it's because, although we were intrigued by what the beatniks were doing, we were really the first *suburban* generation. After the war, the suburbs were created by ex-GIs, with government money, and suddenly middle-class people were more isolated than they had ever been before. Home was a box with a nuclear family in it, held together by raging tensions and resentments, who then filed into a capsule called *the car* to go to a shopping mall that was covered and no longer visible from the streets—these were the people who had to create the next generation of bohemia! They did it by stressing *pleasure*, and it was called being hippie. After that, and after "punk," the links with the culture of poverty were completely severed. Studio 54—people talk about it as a glamorous place, right? But really, the energy of Studio 54 came from preposterous class mixing. It was Liza Minnelli dancing with a black bicycle messenger. It was people getting in not because of who their families were or because of their education but because of how connected they were, either visually or behaviorally, to *pleasure*.

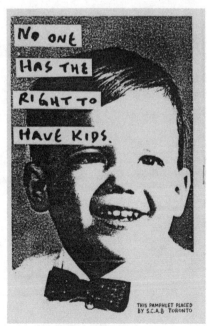

As far as I'm concerned, that was the last great urban moment for pleasure, bohemia, class interpenetration. The Reagan '80s saw the return of the white bourgeoisie into the city, the boutiquing of the city, all the minorities pushed to the periphery—what's called the *donut model*, where instead of having this concentrated mass of anger in places like Harlem or

S.C.A.B. propaganda

Watts, you now had them all *dispersed* so that their anger couldn't congeal and cause trouble. There's no contact between classes, which is a terrible situation for an artist. An artist needs collision with other classes, he needs to be an adventurer. It was the same thing with homosexuality— *that* was a *class* adventure. It was the doctor taking care of the homeless street kid; it was somebody from a white, middle-class home venturing to Harlem, and sleeping with one black stud after another; it was total interpenetration of classes. Homosexuality was a wonderful adventure, based on that kind of rule-breaking. *That* you can call queer. Queer is not discussing strategies, politics, or points of view at the university.

6

LET'S GET BACK TO GAY LIBERATION
AIDS ACTIVISM AND BEYOND

Joanna Brown: When I first joined ACT UP I was coming out of the anarchist movement, which was mostly people yabbering in church basements, theorizing and not *doing* jack shit. At the same time it was very straight; and when I brought up, y'know, *I think I'm queer*, I was told *that's just bourgeois ideology. We can't have that.* Then I started reading about ACT UP. And I was like, *Wow, these people are really* doing *shit—they're, like, tying themselves to members of Congress, I want to go to one of* their *meetings!* But even at ACT UP meetings, while I really appreciated the political work, and I got really involved and really liked the direct-action approach, *socially* I didn't fit it at all.

Poster from the Silence = Death Project, 1987

I was a queer who liked punk rock, and besides my girlfriend Carolyn there really weren't any others.

Jayne County: I, for one, loved ACT UP. I'm not one of those people who say, *No, you have to be nice; you have to do it the right way.* You really have to make a noise. You have to cause some trouble. You have to get attention. If you don't yell and scream, no one's going to listen to you,

Demonstration on women's AIDS issues at the Sixth International AIDS conference in San Francisco, June 22, 1990. Photo by Daniel Nicoletta

they'll just overlook you and move on to the next thing. You have to say, *Hold on, wait a fucking minute*—and it gets people's attention. I think more gay people should be more vocal, even at the cost of getting beat up or whatever. There has to come a point when you open your mouth and stomp your feet.

Eileen Myles: I was peripheral to ACT UP. It was just, like—the speech-making, the fighting for the mic, the egos . . . but the *theater* of ACT UP was brilliant. It was theater people that *started* it. So the notion of what an "action" was—it was taking the language of the avant-garde and putting it into politics.

Silas Howard: The actions were performative and messy—we were really into blood and piss, everything was about the body . . . because blood was *dangerous* then. I remember actions like putting painted-red handprints on homophobic churches—all these different performances, and the graffiti and all of that. That was, before homocore, my first entry point into San Francisco.

Jon Ginoli: One of the things that I did as soon as I got to San Francisco was join ACT UP, The AIDS Coalition to Unleash Power, which was a

The Sixth International AIDS conference in San Francisco, June 22, 1990. Photo by
Dan Nicoletta

leading protest group, very grassroots. Back then we were fighting the
first George Bush, who'd followed Reagan in his lack of response to the
AIDS crisis, which was blatant homophobia—saying, pretty much, *We
don't care if you die*. There were people like Jesse Helms, the senator from
North Carolina, who would battle over every gay issue. It was pretty safe
in the mainstream to be homophobic. So I came here and I got involved
in ACT UP, and I had no musical ambitions. But ACT UP San Francisco
split into two factions near the end of 1990 and by the beginning of '91
had kind of fallen apart.

Sarah Schulman: With ACT UP, the divisions were entirely about class
and race and access to power, and they were inevitable. At the beginning of AIDS, everybody with AIDS was equal because there were no
treatments. As soon as ACT UP forced the creation of treatments then
the inequality showed, because only certain people could get them. And
when those people could get them, they lost interest in the people who
couldn't get them.

Glenn Belverio: Around 1991 I was still in ACT UP, and at that point ACT
UP was being infiltrated by a lot of other political groups. There was this
group of women artists called WAC—Women's Action Committee—and

basically they were these bourgeois women artists who were bitter because their work wasn't being shown as much in galleries as men's work was. Their theory was that sexism was to blame—but it was a bit homophobic, as they would say things like, *Gay men can flirt with the curators, the art scene is run by gay men, and women are excluded . . .* So they would come to ACT UP, like, *We're organizing a protest at Barnes and Noble because there's this new book out—it's like* Mein Kampf. *It's Camille Paglia's* Sexual Personae. And my friends, who were more forward-thinking—we were all more interested in, *What does Camille Paglia have to say? She's a lesbian, she's pro-pornography . . .* and when these women in WAC stood up and said they wanted to protest against a *book*—that's when I was like *I'm done here. This is completely Stalinist. Like, you want to suppress free speech? The publication of a book?*

A year later I went to a book signing for Camille Paglia's book *Sex, Art, and American Culture.* And I went up to her and said—and I wasn't in drag—but I said, *I did a show, Glennda Orgasm. I'm a drag queen, I love Elizabeth Taylor, and I love the essay that you wrote about her.* So immediately we became friends. Then she called me and said we should do a video together—walk around downtown and talk about pornography. And that's when I really broke away from the movement because everybody in ACT UP, and these feminist activists, they were horrified. They considered me like Trotsky, like I had betrayed the revolution.

Dennis Cooper: It was this idea that the homosexual identity should be at the center of everything and we should all subsume our own individualities and our own eccentricities for the cause. It's a standard baby-Marxist kind of thing. And y'know, I wasn't interested in it. People like me were seen as doing weird, self-indulgent, difficult work at a time when—I curated a show with Richard Hawkins called *Against Nature* that was deliberately against the idea that one's work needed to further the cause. And it was eccentric and decadent and we were attacked left and right. It was like, *There's no time for this. This is war. We have no time to fritter away on this decadence.* And what am I going to say to that? I was really not liked by them. They would give all these awards and I would get like, the Most Horrible Person in the World award from some wing of Queer Nation.

Jon Ginoli: What I'd seen with ACT UP was that a few activists could really push the envelope. ACT UP did a lot of protests, a lot of actions that were angry but also funny, and I could see that by pushing the envelope they were getting people who weren't as radical to sort of come in behind them, and then they didn't seem so radical anymore. It was like, when you had activists doing the weird shit out on the edge, then you could get people who weren't as radical or committed or whatever to feel that they could accept those ideas more easily.

Sarah Schulman: The stronger your left is, the more credibility your center has. If you don't have a left, your center *is* the left and then they have no credibility. So if you look at ACT UP—at the time of the AIDS crisis, an idea like gay marriage was basically absurd. No one thought it was possible, and really people didn't think it was desirable either. But when you have ACT UP going into St. Patrick's Cathedral and disrupting mass, and people are realizing, *Wow, these people are serious, and they're going to violate all of these structures that we've created.* Suddenly gay marriage looks *great*, because it's assimilative. But if there hadn't been this left wing, that center would not seem palatable to the dominant culture. So you always have to have a left, or an *extreme* left, so that the center has some kind of credibility. The moment that we're living in now, there *is* no left. So the center moves very far to the right, because it's not dynamic.

Deke Nihilson: When you're the most radical person who speaks out in the room, what you do is you make space for people who would want to say something, but don't want to be the first person to say it. Because they don't want to be the outsider. And when you plant that stake way far out, they can say, *well . . . I'm not sure I agree with* that, *but I do think . . .* and suddenly that space that you've made starts filling. I think that was a good part of what queercore was, and what queercore continues to do— it pushes that boundary to make that space, so someone that doesn't feel like a Stonewall rioter can still say, *well, maybe I'm not going to lock the police in the bar and set it on fire, but I basically agree with these people.* And suddenly you have a crowd that you can make some solidarity with and start making an agenda and pushing things further.

Jon Ginoli: After ACT UP broke up I still wanted to do some kind of activism. There was Queer Nation, which was less AIDS-focused; they did things like kiss-ins. But I wanted to do some kind of activism that sort of picked up where ACT UP had left off, and I thought, *What about* *my gay band idea*? After being in San Francisco for a couple of years I felt like I wanted to do more cultural activism. I thought that Pansy Division could push an envelope in the same way that ACT UP did.

Jody Bleyle: There was a sense at the end of the '80s that the movement was getting a little complacent. People started Queer Nation to be direct-action oriented, doing really radical, creative, direct actions. And the neon stickers were just *everywhere*. It was really good PR; everyone wanted to wear the Queer Nation stickers. Lots of straight people were plastered in Queer Nation stickers.

Johnny Noxzema: I mean, I liked their T-shirts. They had a nice T-shirt. But I don't know what else they did in Canada, really.

Eileen Myles: Queer Nation, of course, took the next step, which was gender. ACT UP was specifically about AIDS, and Queer Nation was everything else—*and* AIDS. It was the next step in queering who we were as a community—*including* women, *including* bisexuals, *including* trans people. Obviously the circus tent was getting bigger, and in a way it was big enough for everybody to come—straight people, y'know, whoever *wanted* to be a part of it. Which was so smart. And that was actually the moment where Homocore—Homocore and Queer Nation were really simultaneous.

Deke Nihilson: Some people were doing ACT UP and felt like the first thing was to try and save our dying. Some people felt like . . . y'know, I was a teenager in the late '80s, and I grew up thinking that I was going to die of AIDS because that's what being gay meant, was to die of AIDS. And there was a strain of thought that said, it's important to fight for the sick among us, but it's also important to have a life. Here and now. We can't just be reduced to dying of AIDS, we have to have our own culture, our own spaces, our own movements; our own positive parts of living too. And that's where I think groups like Queer Nation came from. It was a much more proactive agenda; it said, *OK, let's get back to gay liberation*—and by "gay" I mean lesbian, gay, transsexual, intersex, questioning, queer, whatever—the whole slew. And this was back when there was a debate about whether the word *queer* was appropriate to use. I always preferred it, as sort of a catchall.

Justin Vivian Bond: Queer Nation was a relatively diverse organization, and it was all about queer visibility. Because at that time you couldn't— they wouldn't show men kissing on TV, they wouldn't show lesbians kissing on TV, they wouldn't show a lot of things. The only outlet was these talk shows like Phil Donahue or Oprah. I was on Montel Williams—crossdressers who marry was the theme that day. And I went on, I'd married a lesbian Elvis impersonator, and we went on and talked about gender and that sort of thing. But that was the only outlet in the national media.

In 1995 the cocktail came along that started lengthening people's lives again. People were living longer with AIDS. People who thought they were going to die in a week were suddenly granted a reprieve, so there was a lot of recalibration—the way that messed with your head, especially if you were a person with AIDS who knew and had done everything to prepare for death. And all of a sudden you might not die; you were getting better.

So people reacted to that in many, many different ways. Some people went completely off the rails and became very hedonistic, did a lot of drugs, because they had survivor's guilt or they were so traumatized by what they had been through. Other people became extremely conservative, and said, *OK, now we're going to start with making it normal to be queer, and we're going to introduce gay marriage as the number-one priority for the gay community*. So everybody reacted in different ways, but the upshot of it was that people were no longer out in the streets screaming in the way that they'd been before; and people were reintegrating—*normalizing*, whatever *that* means.

7

FREAKS ON THE EDGES
THE WEST COAST SCENE
(LATE 1980S–MID 1990S)

Larry Livermore: Before Pansy Division was a band—I mean, Jon Ginoli was calling it Pansy Division, but it was basically just him and a guitar and a backing tape. But the minute I heard of it I said, *Yes, this is something that has to happen.* I think we'd already been doing *Homocore* for a while by then, and I'd been reading *J.D.s* from up in Toronto and few other zines; but yeah, I said *we need to do something that's in-your-face.* So I went to see Jon and I said, *Get a band and you've got a record label, because I really want to put out your records.* I felt it was important. I don't think that they ever quite reached the level that I hoped they would, and if they didn't, I think one of the main reasons is that that they were a bit too one-pointed—it was all about being gay. After a few years they started trying to broaden their

Homocore no. 7

Pansy Division flyer for show at
Klubstitute

Pansy Division's "Homosapien" 7"
(Artwork by Anonymous Boy)

Flyer for Pansy Division/Team Dresch
show

subject matter, but I think by then it was a little late. A lot of the songs were really clever, cute lyrics and catchy melodies, but it's like, *We're gay, we're gay* . . . you can only take that subject so far. But I think, at that point, that needed to happen. It's a shame that they didn't move on to a bigger level, because they were a really good band and they deserved to. But they were kind of the pioneers. In early punk there were gay members of lots of bands, sometimes multiple gay members, but I don't remember anybody ever saying, *Oh, that gay band*. People didn't think about it, that was San Francisco in the '70s. By the '80s and '90s it had become a different thing.

Jon Ginoli: The second show that Pansy Division ever did was at a place called the End Up. There was a club night happened there called Klubstitute, which was this floating club that happened at different times in different bars, put on by a troupe of artists, activists, drag queens, performers—misfit queers. At that point I didn't have a band; it was just me and an electric guitar. A couple of guys who I didn't even know said, *You need dancers*, so they came up and danced on stage, which was very effective. Anyway, we were on the bill with Tribe 8. And part of the reason I wanted to do the band was because I felt like I'd been waiting for a long time for a gay band to appear. I knew that there were people who were gay doing music, I don't need to read the list; but nobody was *out*. No one, even people you think were out, was out. They were understood to be out, but they weren't *out*. There was nobody saying, *I'm gay and I'm playing this music*, or, *I'm gay, fuck you.*

Extra Fancy came later; The Screamers didn't have any records out, although I'd heard about them; I didn't know that The Dicks were gay—I knew of the band, but I wasn't really into hardcore. So a lot of the gay aspects of punk rock were kind of hidden, you had to be in the know. In Champaign I knew this girl who would follow bands around; she came back from following Hüsker Dü around, and she was like, *Did you know that two-thirds of Hüsker Dü are gay?* I said, *Well, it has to be the guy with the moustache*—and she was like, *No, it's the other two . . . Really? OK . . .* But it wasn't being addressed. I knew we weren't the first gay rockers, but everybody was too ashamed to speak about it, they were worried about killing their careers. I wanted to be out; I thought, *Someone should be out and if no one is going to be out* we'll *be out.*

I mean, the only people who I knew were out were people like Sylvester and Jimmy Sommerville. Which I have respect for, but it's not my music. I've always had an aversion to gay club dance music, and I did before I even knew that I was gay. I had my own tastes that I'd grown up with and developed, and when I encountered gay culture—there was this body of work that was considered gay culture, and the idea was, *If you're gay, this is what you like.* I checked it out, listened to it, and I just didn't like it very much. I had the things I was really interested in—at that time punk and new wave were fairly new and I was really into it. But that was like kryptonite to most of the gay people that I met.

I had been waiting for a band like Pansy Division to come along, and that's really why Chris and I formed it. We just thought, *Well, someone has got to come out along and do it*; and no one came along and did it, so we came along and did it. It turned out that other people had the same idea at the same time—like Tribe 8, who are really great parallel to Pansy

Division. They're girls, but they're tougher than us boys. They had a different set of issues, but there were parallel issues. We used to say that they were kind of The Stooges to our Ramones. And I think that Tribe 8 really has not been recognized for their contributions. Pansy Division was bigger, we were more commercial, we get credit, but Tribe 8 don't. Which I think is a real shame.

Lynn Breedlove: I was jumping up and down, yelling the words to the first song I ever wrote—that was "Manipulate"—and my friend was like, *That's pretty funny, you should start a band! You should form a band, learn some more songs, and play at my birthday party in five days.* So I went home, and I said to my girlfriend at the time, so Cheryl says I should start a band, but I don't know anybody that plays music. And she was like, *Well, there's Lynn Flipper who plays guitar, and there's Kat who plays drums . . .*

So I called them up. They were like, *Yeah, let's do it!* Me and Silas were newly sober, so we were like, *Lots of energy, yeah!* We piled up these mattresses in Silas's back room, on the walls and on the floor, trying to soundproof it. And we just made up five songs, and then we set up at the birthday party, and we played the five songs. There must have been ten or fifteen dykes there, and they were like, *Yeah!* And Silas (who was Lynn Flipper at the time) had his shirt off—it wasn't me, Silas was the first one that did that. Everybody was like, *Yeah!* And then they wanted more, so we had to play the whole five songs all over again. And then it just went from there . . . Everybody was just dying for dykes jumping up and down and yelling about being dykes; it didn't matter that we sucked, they were too happy. And then Leslie Mah was there; we were like, *We need a bass player. Who plays bass?* Leslie was all shy . . .

Tantrum: We weren't thinking in terms of doing anything revolutionary, y'know. Everybody wanted to have fun, and make some music, learn to play their instruments. There was no big picture, like, *We're forming this revolutionary thing.*

Lynn Breedlove: It was totally about fun. We weren't in any kind of political space at the time; we were just jumping up and down, wanting to have fun—we *were* having fun, being ourselves. Valencia Street at that time, in the early '90s—if you walked down Valencia from 24th Street to

16th Street, you would see at least five dykes with mohawks and facial piercings walking out their front doors, people you *knew*—just, like, all queers, all the time. It was what I'd call a dyke renaissance. It was kind of like Paris in the 1930s. It was crazy. We were forming all kinds of little gangs, like, *Let's do a dyke-only sober space called Whiptail Lizard Lounge! And let's meet every week, and have anarchist meetings, and then let's have play parties and pierce each other's titties and crossdress and be weird. And let's open an all-dyke café and start an all-dyke band, an all-dyke spoken-word troupe!*—and on and on and on. It was all just happening, it was this hotbed of dyke revolution that was happening in the early '90s, when we started.

Kaia Wilson: Back then we called each other dykes.

Silas Howard: We called each other dykes because *lesbian* was more folk-based—y'know folk music, Michigan Womyn's Music Festival . . .

Lynn Breedlove: Our first name wasn't Tribe 8; it was Venus Envy. We thought that was *so* brilliant and original. Well, it wasn't; there were a million things called Venus Envy, people had columns called Venus Envy . . . There was this lesbian band called Venus Envy that got really mad, and they had their *lawyer* send us a fucking letter. Because for our first show we made a poster that said Venus Envy; we had our friends bring

Cover of Tribe 8's "Pig Bitch" 7"

panties to throw at us—it was a warehouse party, y'know. I don't know *how* they found out about us, but these old lesbians got pissed off. They were like, *You can't use our name. We're Venus Envy and we're going places, and you're not going to steal our name!* We were like, *OK, whoa! . . . Stupid name anyway. We don't care* . . . So that's when we came up with Tribe 8. Of course, Venus Envy was never heard from again, as far as I know. We were in different realms, anyway, so I don't think there was much chance that we were going to be competing with each other.

Jody Bleyle: I put together a show for Tribe 8 in Portland, in this recycling warehouse that I worked at—my band Lovebutt opened for them. They rolled up in their van with, like, two motorcycles following them, and they opened the van door and, like, four dogs got out . . . they were so tough. I fucking love Tribe 8. That show that we played at the warehouse was one of the best shows I've ever played.

We started an all-dyke band because we were dykes and we just needed each other. For me, I was at a point when I felt like . . . I remember, my friend Anna—who became my sister in love, she did the *Free to Fight* album with me, and we were in Lovebutt together—I remember one day burying my head in her bosom and crying and saying, *I love you guys, and I love playing music with you, but I feel like I have to find some dykes to play with, and I just don't know if I'm ever going to find them.* And she was like, *You* will. *You've said it and you will.*

Shortly after that, my band Hazel was playing a show in Olympia. Our bass player Brady had gone to Evergreen College and worked at the Smithfield in Olympia. We were walking in the alley behind the Capitol Theatre, and Donna was coming the other way; and he was like, *You have to meet Donna, I worked with her at the Smithfield!* I already had Donna's 7", from Dangermouse—I loved that 7". So we pretty much talked about starting Team Dresch right then and there. I said, *I want to be in a band like Tribe 8. I want to be in a band with dykes. I want to roll up in a van with a bumper sticker that says* DON'T LAUGH, YOUR DAUGHTER MAY BE IN THIS VAN, *like they did.* I didn't necessarily want that many dogs in the van . . .

Donna Dresch: When she said that, I was like, *Oh shit!*

Jody Bleyle: I mean, I'd never lived in San Francisco. In Portland we were more like—we had a little hippie, a little punk . . . we weren't all, like, leather fucking studs and pit bulls like Tribe 8. We lived in a small town. When they rolled up it was just exciting!

When I met Donna and I said, *I want to be in a band like Tribe 8* she probably thought that I wanted to be in a really hardcore punk band. But that's not the part of Tribe 8 that I loved, I didn't really listen to that kind of music. My favorite musician is Joni Mitchell. But I loved their dykeness, y'know. I just wanted to be around dykes. I felt like I needed to go more full-frontal—full-frontal dykeness.

Lynn Breedlove: I guess we were calling it homocore; Tom Jennings was calling it homocore because G.B. Jones and Bruce LaBruce were calling it homocore, they had that whole thing going out in Canada. And then we coopted that. Tom Jennings was living in this warehouse with Diet Popstitute—they were a bunch of fucking crazy drag queens and fags. They were hilarious, the Popstitutes. Tom had his zine, *Homocore*. And then Deke Nihilson had an offshoot of that, a zine called *Three Dollar Bill*. And Matt Wobensmith, I think, coined the term *queercore*—to *my* knowledge, the first time I remember hearing it was from him, for his record label Outpunk.

The Popstitutes

1 Diet Popstitute
2 Tyler Bob is the bashed
3 Ramor Von Popstitute died for our sins (Club DNA Easter 89)
4 Ramor Von Popstitute (Gay Day Parade 90)
5 Diet Popstitute
6 (Yes On 'S' benefit 89)
7 Zaza and Fruit Fly (Club DNA Easter 89)

Photos Tyler Bob Ingenue Popstitute

Who's who of The Popstitutes

Jody Bleyle: I heard the term *homocore* from Donna Dresch, because she had lived in the Shred of Dignity warehouse, and she had been part of the *Homocore* zine and knew the Fifth Column people so she kind of turned me on to that scene.

Silas Howard: I heard it from Tom Jennings, and all the zines that they were writing around that time. They were, like, *naming* this movement that was happening around the clubs—Diet Popstitute, shows that were happening at Gilman Street . . . basically, it was like a gaggle of homos going to all the straight shows and looking across the room and spotting each other. But we weren't *gathered* yet; we were just sort of spotting each other among the crowd.

Tom Jennings: There was this layer of arty weirdos, and we were less concerned with who was gay or not than having a cohort to hang out with. There was the Popstitutes and queer weirdos like the Radical Faeries. The Radical Faeries had a lot of queer punk people go in and out of it. At first they weren't particularly welcoming and some of them didn't like us, but some of them really did—they liked the new energy. They were always building hippie shrines out in the woods. Then someone did a couple of punk ones—instead of being these hyper-symmetrical, reverent things, with flowers and candles, they were, like, broken glass and records and spit . . .

We were having fun, making mischief. We were bored by gay bars. The Popstitutes were doing weirdo theater. They were bad but hilariously fun—an annoying band that would come and make a big mess with stuffed animals and sex toys and duct tape and really awful music. They started a club called Klubstitute, which spawned a lot of great stuff in San Francisco—they started theater groups, they would do these open mic nights, and their approach was, like, grade-school dorky. It was so refreshing. They were anticool. The cool kids were the pretty ones who got laid in the gay bars and were all sort of conformist, and we were just weirdos.

Jody Bleyle: When we started Team Dresch, Donna and I would say that we felt like freaks among freaks. We didn't fit into the gay world, but we didn't feel like we fit into the punk world or the rock world either. So if you're a freak among freaks, you definitely want to find that other freaks among freaks. I think there were a lot of people here and there doing that.

Phranc: I was up in San Francisco, and a friend and I went to this concert put on at the Women's Building by QTIP, Queers Together in Punkness. I didn't know any of the bands; we just decided to go. And Team Dresch took the stage, and I just remember standing there and *crying*. I could not believe how moved I was. It felt like it was all happening again—all this passion, and politics, and *music*. I felt moved like I hadn't in years.

Jody Bleyle: When I saw Phranc play for the first time—I walked into the Women's Building in San Francisco, and Phranc was on stage wearing a flannel shirt and a baseball hat, holding her guitar and sound-checking, and tears just started running down my face. I didn't realize why at first, but I remember driving home after the show, and just thinking . . . I don't think that I'd ever seen a woman older than me—I mean, Phranc is only, like, ten years older than me—but I don't think I'd ever seen an adult woman just, like, looking butch and wearing a baseball hat, with a crewcut . . .

Lynn Breedlove: We definitely felt like there was a movement. When we were on tour—the amazing thing about being a queer band on tour in the '90s was that you were in this little bubble with all these other queers. And you're so fucking grateful that you're in this van with four other queers because you're traveling through this cultural wasteland, and there *are* no fucking queers. When you pull up to the club, and there are the fucking queers standing out front—you can *see* them, y'know, they've got the funny colored hair, they've got the facial piercings, they've got the mohawk, whatever, the combat boots—you're like, *There's our people—yes!* And you have two or three other bands and they're all a bunch of queers, singing about being queer, jumping up and down, and they're all terrible, or great, or whatever—terribly great—and you're like, *Yes! We're all doing this thing together.*

Jody Bleyle: Donna told me how at the Shred of Dignity warehouse, they would tell people—*Come! You, person that doesn't live in San Francisco that's trapped in this terrible family situation—come stay here!* And of course people did. It was the same with us, we would say in interviews, *Come to Portland. There's a place for you!* Now I would never say something like that, because I take everything more seriously—I'd think, *I can't* actually *take care of them.* But at the time we were young and we wanted other kids like us to know that they had a family.

Cookie: From my perspective it definitely seemed like there was a movement. There was Matt Wobensmith with Outpunk records, which was something I was really excited about—I would write him letters and get 7"s in the mail, and that would totally make my week, getting packages like that. There was the *There's a Faggot in the Pit* 7", then there was the *Dyke in the Pit* 7". Those came out—it seemed to me like there was a real convergence of that stuff happening at the time.

Jody Bleyle: Queercore *was* a movement—a social movement, a socio-political movement really. It brought a lot of cultural visibility to the gays, to the queers, to the freaks. And that definitely helps the people working on the political angles—political representation, civil rights issues, people that are doing the technical work to move those things forward. They need the freaks on the edges doing the cultural work. That was us, the freaks on the edges.

Without that cultural visibility, without these visions of ourselves and sounds of ourselves, we don't even know that we *exist,* much less that we deserve rights and political representation. I mean, no one starts by saying, *I wish there were a gay senator;* they're just like, *I want to make out with a girl. Are there other girls that do that? What will I be like when I'm forty? What will I be like when I'm seventy? Is there anyone else out there? What do people do? What can I do?* Possibilities, y'know. You want to see the possibilities. You have to know you have a reason to live before you can care whether you can get married.

8

BODIES COLLIDING
MACHISMO (AND MACHISMA) IN THE PUNK SCENE

Jayne County: At the height of punk, admitting you were gay was not a good idea. It was like saying you weren't rough enough or tough enough to be a punk. Which is ironic, because in prison *punk* means the boy who gets fucked up the ass. A lot of the punks didn't know that, they had no idea where the word came from. It was made up by *Punk* magazine to sell papers. The Ramones got upset. They didn't even want to be called punks; they said, *What is this punk shit? We're a rock 'n' roll band*.

I remember a gig in New Jersey—we got there and the place was run by these real heavy, Mafia-type people. I have a song called "If You Don't Want to Fuck Me Baby, Fuck Off," and when I did that song, some of the rough guys in the audience were really enraged that I was saying *fuck* and saying it in front of their girlfriends. But they didn't attack me; they attacked my manager. I had already sung "Storm the Gates of Heaven" and masturbated with a statue of the Virgin Mary. These were all Catholic Mafia members—and I had insulted them horribly. By the time I was singing *fuck off*, I looked over from the stage and they had my manager Peter Crowley down of the floor and they were kicking the shit out of him. They wouldn't come up on stage and do anything to me; they were those kind of macho guys who didn't want to be seen beating anyone up that was wearing a wig and makeup. It somehow seemed less manly to them, with their overmasculine mentality. But they'd beat up my managers or try to pick a fight with members of my band. A couple times I had glasses thrown at me, or beer poured down my face, stuff like that, but I'd just pick the glass up and throw it back at them. People kind of knew not to do that to me. But there was a lot of homophobia, too; I got into some fights at CBGB.

Larry Livermore: By the end of the '70s and early '80s the first wave of punk, which had been pretty open and accepting to weirdos of all kinds—a lot of that sort of disappeared into drug addiction and loss of interest, and it got replaced by a more violent kind of . . . metal crossover, *speedcore* as they called it. At that point shows became very scary and macho. I remember, my little brother had first turned me on to punk in 1976, but he had lost interest, he was like, *It sucks now.* And I said, *Come on*—this was '84—*just try one more time. I'll take you to the show tonight.* It was this band called Fang. And we went and there was literally blood flying through the air as bodies collided. And my brother said, *I'm never going back to anything like that again.* I didn't, myself, for a couple of years.

Bruce LaBruce: There was a lot of machismo, because of the pit, the mosh pit, and the aggressive music—speedcore, thrash, metal. So, even though it was extremely homoerotic, there was a lot of homophobia as well. It was—we were sort of getting back to the roots of punk. So punk, for us—the original root of the word *punk*, the etymology, was based on jailhouse slang where *punks* were the passive boys in jail who got fucked up the ass. And taking it back even further, *punk* meant the wood that was used as kindling to light fires where fags were burned at the stake. So we were getting back to the original etymology of *punk*. Punk Is Gay was our motto.

Vaginal Davis: All these hot, sexy punk boys slamming half naked . . . that whole Huntington Beach scene with all the boys with the ripped pants. Of course they didn't wear underwear. A lot of people did complain about the macho element that came into the punk scene with the HB years, but on some levels it was very homoerotic because all those boys going out with each other in packs was very homo-y. Very, very homo-y.

Larry-Bob Roberts: At first, every city had a band—there were bands like Ze Whiz Kidz in Seattle, which was Tomata du Plenty, who was later in The Screamers, and who had been involved in the Angels of Light and the Cockettes and brought a queer theatrical sensibility to the scene; there was a band in Washington, DC, called the Nuclear Crayons that was also in that campy, B-52s kind of vein; in New York there was Jayne County, there was the whole Mudd Club scene that had a lot of queer folks, Lance Loud and Kristian Hoffman who were in the Mumps, Klaus Nomi . . . there are plenty of examples. But as things changed, from that artsy era of punk into the more macho, hardcore slam-dancing—when it started to be about loud and fast rather than weird and different, there was a drop-in participation by women and by queer folks. When Queercore came along, it was kind of about reclaiming some of that original spirit.

Brian Grillo: Lock Up was on a small tour through the south—it was Tom Morello and Chris and myself and Vince. And it was a nightmare. We were on tour with a big-hair heavy metal band. They didn't have any idea what to do with us. They were like, *Wow, a really good black guitar player and singer that's gay* . . . David Geffen was like, *You should change the name of the band from Lock Up to something else because it sounds like a leather bar.* It's like, *How would you know that?* Y'know? It was like, *whatever.* I remember one night we were at this club and Tom was like, *Can you get me a coke?* And I was like, *Dude, you can get a coke yourself, we're at the bar.* And he was like, *They won't serve me because I'm black.* And, y'know?—I went through the same thing for being gay. It was terrifying, playing in front of all these audiences where it's like, *Well, I have to go up there and rock out in front of all these people that if they knew what I was would want to kill me.* And I think a lot of anger came out of that.

Tantrum: That was part of the angst that Tribe 8 performed on stage—it was very much a parody of this *cock rock.*

Mykel Board: There's this jock element—these guys who would have been on the football team but somehow got into punk rock. The flying fists . . . it's not that they don't care if they injure somebody—they *try* to hurt somebody. So a band like Tribe 8, where—OK, so you've got all these macho guys who slam around and take their shirts off and show off their pecs; now you've got these mach(a) *girls* who get on stage and take *their* shirts off and show off *their* pecs! Homocore, to me, is exactly that—using homosexuality to make punk.

Scott Free: My trio opened for Tribe 8 at the Fireside Bowl, in 1997 or '98, a Homocore Chicago show. Tribe 8 was famous for their fans—their fans were crazy, they were all women, and they would all take off their

TRIBE EIGHT

Tribe 8 is a relatively new San Francisco band that has been making waves everywhere they play. They've developed quite a reputation as a band with an agenda to be reckoned with. MRR's Matt Smith caught up with them in the Epicenter library for this tantalizing interview.

The band is: Lynn Breedlove - "mouth", Lynn Flipper - guitar, Leslie Mah - guitar, Mahia - bass, Kat - drums.

MRR: How long have you been together?

LF: We've been together for about a year and a half.

LM: And that includes learning how to play our instruments.

MRR: Do you have a statement of purpose? A common goal?

M: We apparently have a statement of purpose. It's this page written by Breedlove.

LM: We've revised it at this point so that it's a little more up-to-date.

MRR: Well, please be brief.

LM: We're validating cultural identity in the underground music scene for dykes. Unison: Dykes.

LF: That wasn't our purpose when we started, but now...

LB: We wanted to get girlfriends.

LF: Our purpose in the beginning was to play at parties, but I think being dykes and playing music is political. It's not like we meant it to be; we just are. But yeah, the way we play our music - the style, and the lyrics that Lynn writes is very political.

M: The fact that we're obviously dykes...

LM: No we're not!

M: Oh, I'm sorry. You're, uh, pretty femme. I mean, just existing as a gay person these days is political.

LM: Well, just to be out and not being closeted is a very political thing. The way you live your life can be a very political statement, if you're not in the mainstream. If you're queer, well, there you are.

LB: If you refuse to conform in any way, and you state that fact in public repeatedly, and shout it, yell it, in spite of the fact that people may be spitting on you...

M: And throwing cans at you...

LB: Booing at you and you insist on doing it anyway... and are confrontational about it, that is like the most militant politics that

an artist can express.

M: being true to It's being really That's what said about us.

MRR: Why talk about with NoFX at Friday

LF: I think for straights didn't like us silent. But these gentlemen were very vocal

It's oneself. honest. someone

don't you your show Gilman last night?

we've played before that and were si- fine young the crowd about it. Like

REVOLUTION GIRL-STYLE

"Fuck you, dykes" as get up there. slammed to from what I They were en-

LB: I don't the same peo- slamming. I problem was...

LF: I watched

you fuckin' soon as we They also every song could see. joying it. know that ple were think the the same

two guys yell "fuckin' dykes" and slam and then yell "you fuckin dykes".

All: *laughter*

LF: They were definitely the same guys.

LB: But it's a testosterone problem: "We have to slam into each other, we have to beat the fuck out of each other, and we're forced to flip these people off, especially if they will not fuck us. They have pussies, and won't allow us to put our dicks in those pussies." It's like a turret syndrome: "Fuck you! Fuck you! Fuck you!" (*waving extended middle finger wildly*)

M: I think we handled it pretty well.

LB: This guy grabbed Mahia's pussy in the middle of "Lesbophobia". This was after "Frat Pig", before which we made a big speech about how we deal with gang rape, which is with gang castrate. When we first talked about gang rape, all of the men in the crowd jumped up and down and cheered "Yippee, we're all for gang rape, what a great weekend past-time". And we said the way we dealt with that was gang castrate. That started getting their blood boiling a little bit. And then by "Lesbophobia", they were just so afraid, one of them just reached out and grabbed Mahia by the cunt. At this, she proceeded to throw the bass down, the whole song had to stop while she punched the guy in the face. Six girls jumped on the guy, jumped up and down on him, kicked him in the balls, and threw him out.

LF: And we stopped playing, which was good. We just started yelling into the mike. We had the power position at that point, and we got to say what we needed to say.

LB: It was a really good opportunity to speak directly to the people we're always singing about. I realized that all of these songs I'm writing are totally abstract. I'm like - I realize that homophobia exists, I may encounter that on one level here and there. I hear people talk about their experiences, and I read about shit in the paper, and I write about it. But when you're faced with the actual mob psychology, you shit. And I got to address this instead of preaching to the converted like we normally do. All of

Photos: Stacie Quijas

Tribe 8 in *Maximum Rocknroll*

shirts and jump around. The Fireside Bowl would get really hot, and so . . . their set ended, and I remember walking through the crowd and it turned into this very surreal image—this *sea* of naked women, with the steam floating up, it almost felt like slow-motion, and even as I'm walking through I'm like, *Oh my god, I will* never *experience this again*. The energy that Tribe 8 brought—their fans were amazing, but it was definitely an all-women thing. That was the point.

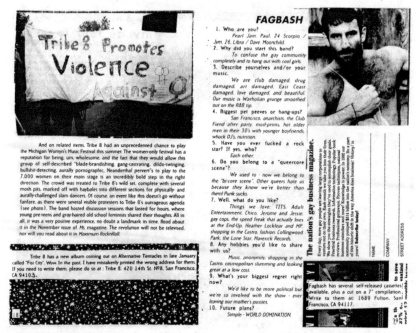

Tribe 8 in *Outpunk*

Lynn Breedlove: We got into trouble in a couple of places. In Bloomington we played this all-ages show, and right about the time that I was chopping off the rubber dick or I was getting a blowjob or something, some *mom* came in to collect her child, her fifteen-year-old, and dragged her out by the ear. And then complained. The place almost got shut down, their funding almost got cut off . . . and then the whole mayoral race for the next six months, the campaigns were all about this place, and Tribe 8, and how terrible things were happening to the youth in Bloomington. So . . . we were banned there.

We were also banned in P-Town. We were playing at this—City Hall or something, some kind of fancy, founding-fathers place. The cops came in, and I had my shirt off; and somebody came up and said, *The cops are going to pull the plug unless you put your shirt back on*. And I always seized the opportunity to make a speech about censorship when something like that happened. Like, *It's totally fine for dudes, but it's not OK for me? What about my dick? My dick doesn't mean anything? I could put someone's eye out with that—but no, it's the titties that are dangerous? OK, whatever*. And then we jumped right into this cop-hating song called "Power Boy." I'm sure the cops didn't even catch on, but we thought it was hilarious.

We didn't care if straight guys approved, we didn't care if straight guys came out to the show. We loved it when fags came to the show, and if they wanted to come up front and be in the mosh pit, that was great. And we'd say, *If you're a dude in the front, and you're in the mosh pit, you better be a fag, otherwise bad things will happen to you.* And we had the power of the mic, and we'd go, *Look at that guy throwing his elbow in girls' faces! That's bad, dude. You shouldn't be doing that . . .* And dykes would just jump on the guy and beat the crap out of him and throw him to the back.

We were, like, high on our own bullshit; but, y'know, it was *new*. We had just experienced the '80s, which was all lipstick lesbian; the '70s had been, like, this super-serious, political, all-penetration-is-rape kind of feminism; and we were on the break of this third wave. It was like, *We're doing something different here. We're not lesbians, we're* dykes.

Donna Dresch: We got harassed onstage—*often*. But then people at the shows were like, *That dude's an asshole. We need to take care of it.* So we also had a posse. We had the assholes and the posse. Which was really liberating for the people in the posse, to be like, *We're going to take our own space.*

Jody Bleyle: Every show we played had to be an all-ages show or, if it was at a bar, it had to be promoted as a queer show. Because we actively wanted queer people to come to the shows. I mean, we wanted *everybody* to come to the shows—but we also wanted them to know that it was a queer space. Like, it's on the table: you fuck around with us at the show, we are going to come down on you hard. And we did. It did happen, a lot.

9

GROOVY UNDERWEAR
PANSY DIVISION FLIRTS WITH
THE MAINSTREAM (1994)

Adam Rathe: A huge moment for queercore was when Green Day took Pansy Division on tour with them—and, y'know, they had trepidation about going through the south. I was shocked to hear that one of the few places they had trouble in, where a promoter asked Green Day to take Pansy Division off the bill, was the place where I grew up, a suburb of Washington, DC, which always felt very liberal and accepting and open-minded to me. This promoter at a venue down the street from where I grew up said to Green Day, *We don't want this band playing. We don't want our kids seeing that.* Luckily Green Day, who were the most famous band in the world at that time, were able to say, *We can play anywhere we want; this band is going on.* But it was shocking to realize that something I thought was true about my own life wasn't; that there were still people out there who would try to *stop* something like that—Pansy Division opening a punk show, that that would rile someone up was surprising.

Jon Ginoli: When Green Day reached that major label level they wanted to show where they came from, so they were taking all these different Lookout! bands on tour with them. They'd taken others on tour before us, and different ones after us. But we happened to be on the tour when they broke. That was the biggest thing in popularizing us. We *never* expected to play fifteen-thousand-seat arenas. We thought that 150 people was a really big crowd.

When I formed the band with Chris, we did not expect—our ambitious goal was to have a band, make a record or two, have the chance to go on vacations every year from work, and go to New York or Chicago or wherever and play in the few big cities where maybe people would get it. When I started the band I was thirty-two; so I thought, *I'm not doing this for the kids; I'm doing this for gay guys in their twenties and thirties who just don't buy the whole argument that gay culture is this limited.* And then it kind of went the other way, and we got way more popular than we ever expected. If we'd thought, *Let's do a band that will get popular and sell thousands of records,* we *never* would have done it that way! We would have done something different. So it was pretty wonderful to be able to do our own thing and have it take off on some kind of subcultural level.

Larry Livermore: I was Pansy Division's label at the time, and I had been Green Day's label up until then, so I'm in some sense responsible for putting them together. I mean, Green Day represented— ahead of their time, too—a kind of punk consciousness. They're not gay; but they knew it wasn't right to pick on somebody for being different in any way. I think they got a big kick out of Pansy Division's lyrics, because some of them were pretty funny, and they got an even bigger kick out of shocking their suburban fans.

Pansy Division on tour with Green Day

Green Day, when they suddenly went from being an underground band to one of the biggest mainstream bands, it was hard on them mentally. They were used to this very close-knit family at Gilman Street, where you could say and do almost anything, and suddenly they're playing in these arenas to fairly generic audiences. And Green Day said, *They need to know we're not like one of those mainstream rock acts. We're something different, and if you doubt that, here's Pansy Division.* Sometimes Pansy Division got a pretty rough welcome—but not always. A lot of Pansy Division's audiences were straight punk kids—it always bewildered me, they had more straight fans than gay ones. But other times they got stuff thrown at them.

Jon Ginoli: Yeah, they threw things at us. But they threw things at Green Day too! It was not out of hatred but just people going wild. Coins can cause a lot of damage; I had dents on my guitar. All of us bled a few times. I remember someone launched an entire Big Gulp drink at me in Los Angeles that completely drenched me. They had to be really strong to throw something that heavy that far—but it got me!

Larry Livermore: Green Day was like, *As long as you can take it, we're proud to have you.* I know that Pansy Division treasure that to this day. And Green Day still remember it too, y'know. It was a pretty awesome thing—I mean, it's not the most heroic thing in the world, but . . . there weren't a whole lot of openly gay bands at that time, and it was a good thing to do. I remember MTV or VH1 or one of those channels made a special on Green Day right after that tour, and it closed with Green Day driving away singing "Groovy Underwear," the Pansy Division song.

Jon Ginoli: We weren't trying to shock people. We were just out there expressing ourselves naturally. We weren't trying to do anything that we weren't already doing for any other audience—except saying a few things about growing up, and things about safe sex. We suddenly had this teenage audience, so we put information about safe sex and condoms in our album and CD booklets, with help numbers for people to call, 800 numbers, talk lines, addresses for local gay groups. And we got a lot of fan mail, people telling us that they had written to these places and called these places, kids telling us what was going on in their high schools. For a band that started out expecting to have a nearly all-gay audience—I think at that point it was probably 80-90 percent straight. We had gay fans at first—and then *all* these straight fans.

Larry Livermore: It bothered me a little bit, it was almost like they were a novelty act. And yet they were serving an important educational purpose. But I remember, there was a queer punk festival in the Mission District around 1995-96. It was well-attended enough; but I remember thinking, *Two blocks away, in the Castro—there are probably thousands of people dancing to club music, house music, whatever they were calling it at the time—and here at the queer punk festival in the Mission there are maybe a hundred people, and half of them are straight.* Like, what is missing here? I was never able to answer that question satisfactorily. In fact, I used to half-tease Pansy Division, like, *Why don't you put more dance beats into your music, so you can cross over and tap into the whole gay scene too—and they can learn something about punk* . . . but they never—I don't think that was in their blood.

10

THE NAME GAME
HOMOCORE VS. QUEERCORE

G.B. Jones: I started out with the name *homocore* because I thought it was funny. It's a play on the word hardcore, and I thought it would be upsetting for people. But because of the kinds of letters I was getting from people writing to *J.D.s*, it became obvious that a certain type of male audience thought it was really about *them*—like, only about gay men. So I thought, *Oh my god, I've got to do something. I have to change the name before it's too late and all these people think it's just about gay guys.* I thought, it's not going to go anywhere if that happens. It's not going to be interesting if it's exclusionary. It can only be valuable if it's *inclusionary*.

Scott Treleaven: There are different cycles within each movement. *Queer* was really primary for the period that I was involved in, the late '90s; and then after that people started embracing the word *gay* again. G.B. coined the term *homocore* at the time because she thought it was funny—*homo* as in homosexual and *core* as in hardcore. *Gaycore* didn't make any sense. *Queercore* sounded better and queercore was more inclusionary. So I think the word kind of generated itself out of necessity.

Larry-Bob Roberts: There was sort of a casting around for terminology at the beginning. I was playing around with words like *pervert*. We were going to reclaim a whole bunch of terms. It wasn't like *queer* was the only word out there. People would reclaim words like *deviant, dyke, fag*; there was a zine called *Fags and Faggotry* that was around early on, I think I saw it listed in *J.D.s*. So people were playing around with all these things, we weren't locked in to just using the word *queer*.

Homocore Rules

Gay Zine Makers Bust a Move

By Dennis Cooper

Dennis Cooper on queercore zines

Bruce LaBruce: We coined the phrase *homocore*, and we didn't use *queer*, we consciously didn't use the word *queer*, because we thought that *queer* had become very politicized or ideological. There was Queer Nation, ACT UP; people were more queer-identified, and we didn't embrace that kind of political orthodoxy. For us, *queer* was too loaded with that kind of political meaning. So we called it homocore, and then other fanzines and other scenes kind of transmuted it into *queercore*. There was a crossover between a kind of gay punk movement and these queer radicals that were within the gay scene. So there was a kind of merger at a certain point. But we always stayed outside of those kind of internecine struggles within the gay world.

Brontez Purnell: I embraced the term *queer* because when I first moved to Oakland, it felt like, *Oh, we can do anything*, but now as the term progresses, I feel it becomes a pissing match for wokeness. But also it was radical to call yourself gay in the '40s, '50s, and '60s—I think that sometimes people that called themselves gay before us did more radical things, sociopolitically, than we do now. I think people think that just because we can change the term, it means that we're this new animal, when actually . . . I know plenty of people that call themselves queer that aren't very cool people at all and actually did not do anything cooler than the history they wish to erase. These days I have so many journalists refer to me as a queer person of color, but now that I'm older I think "person of color" is a term meant to erase black people, specifically because it's an umbrella term because there are things that are very specifically black. Like whenever Beyoncé does something that everyone wants to claim, they'll be like, *Oh she's a woman of color*, but she does very specific black things. Not that I'm a black separatist or a black militant but these umbrella terms are very problematic with the specific struggles of black people or the specific things we had to do to survive. And also what I've noticed is that there's lots of fucking colorism and as a dark-skinned man, I specifically refer to myself these days as a black, old-school homosexual.

Scott Treleaven: It's funny to think about Queer Nation as being politically correct . . . I mean, can you imagine Queer Nation existing at this moment? They wouldn't be PC; they were essentially separatists. Nobody would call it Queer Nation now. Mainstream gays don't want to use the term queer anymore. If you talk about marriage it's *gay marriage*; you don't say *queer marriage*—that would terrify everyone. So *queer* has actually become this marginal word again.

Tom Jennings: This is where histories really just start to piss me off—it's like, *We need to coin terms; we need to label these things!* We didn't call ourselves fucking anything. There was no self-referentialness to this. It was description, not proscription. As far as I know, no one called this movement—this "movement"—*homocore* until it was kind of over, really.

11

WE HAD OUR PHOTOCOPIERS
THE QUEER ZINE EXPLOSION

Larry-Bob Roberts: One of the big inspirations in terms of punk and literature was Dennis Cooper. I first ran across Dennis's writings in the *Men on Men* anthologies, these anthologies of mainstream gay men's writing, but for some reason in the middle of this was his transgressive punk rock thing. Sometimes I think I like Dennis Cooper for the wrong reasons; maybe I just like it because there's punk rock in it, even though there's this other aspect of Dennis's writing where these guys are so drugged out and uncreative, it's sort of the opposite of what the punk scene really was like for me. I'd always been straight edge, I was a straight edge gay punk; and that was part of my rebellion against the mainstream, was not being a drugged-out person.

The other thing—I don't know if we were aware at that time, but Dennis had done his own kind of queer zine called *Little Caesar* that was basically a punk literary magazine that happened ten years before the queer zine scene.

Adam Rathe: Dennis Cooper was critiquing queercore fanzines early on for the *Village Voice*, he wrote some scathing reviews which were great.

Dennis Cooper: I was in University and I decided to quit school and go to England. This was, like, 1976. I wanted to see the whole punk thing that was going on over there. So I came to England for a few months and I went to see whatever bands existed at that point, and sort of looked at what was going on, what kind of zines—like *Sniffin' Glue* and stuff like that. And when I went back to LA I was really inspired to create a magazine or a zine that was focused on poetry but had that kind of punk spirit, because it always seemed like poetry was in these very boring contexts, really "elegant." So that was the spirit behind *Little Caesar*, to kind of tap into that punk spirit and make poetry as popular as I thought it should be. I was just frustrated with how *adult* the whole thing was. I mean, there were some cool magazines that I liked, but mostly it felt like you were visiting some dignitary's house or something when you had a poem in a magazine. And I just didn't see any way for people like myself and my friends that really wanted to shake things up to be able to do that. There was no kind of vehicle or scene. I wrote this manifesto in the first issue that poetry should be, like, we should all be rock stars or whatever. But that was the idea, just to try to create a context where people like myself and people I admired could be in this kind of maga-zine. I was also doing readings at a place called Beyond Baroque, trying to build this scene that had the energy and aesthetic of punk but which was focused, at least initially, on poetry.

Adam Rathe: I think zines were sort of the thing that started it all; the zines are what seemed to catch on first. *J.D.s* is often credited as being the first queercore zine, but before that there was Dr. Smith, also out of Toronto. Tom Jennings started making *Homocore* after an anarchist con-vention in Toronto, Donna Dresch was doing *Chainsaw*, and on the East Coast Erin Smith was making *Teenage Gang Debs*. People were making and trading zines—it was about trading ideas, and that really fostered the community that birthed all the bands.

Brontez Purnell: The first zines I ever came across, I think I was twelve or thirteen years old and *Spin* magazine used to have this classifieds section in the back and I think I was just writing to people off of there. And I used to get these random zines. I made my first zine when I was thirteen or fourteen—*Spandex Press*—No Doubt was in it, kids from my school. It was, like, so "first zine," y'know?

Sarah Schulman: The queer zines have a history—because there was already an underground gay and lesbian and feminist press, and black press. I mean—in 1979 I was a reporter; I was twenty-one years old. I worked for *Woman News*, which was the New York City feminist newspaper; I worked for *Gay Community News*, which was the socialist gay and lesbian newspaper; I worked for the *Guardian*, which was the Marxist weekly newspaper; I worked for the *New York Native*, which was the gay male newspaper. There was a radical black press, there was the *East Village Other*, which was the radical neighborhood press. There was this *huge* alternative print press. And zines come very much out of that.

Milo Miller: Early LGBT publishing was almost zine-like. If you look back to the 1940s and the publications of Lisa Ben—she put out a lesbian newsletter. Lisa Ben was an anagram of *lesbian*. She would type up a bunch of stuff and run off copies on the mimeograph when the boss wasn't looking. And you look at publications like *ONE* magazine, and the *Ladder*, where people were writing about gay and lesbian lives. *ONE* magazine became the subject of a freedom-of-the-press lawsuit—even though there was nothing sexual or erotic in it, it was considered smut because it talked about homosexuality.

Chris Wilde: There is *nothing* sexy about that publication. But in 1953 it was considered obscene material. When one of their issues was seized, they filed suit and it went all the way to the Supreme Court. And they won! That's what ensured the freedom to publish, and send through the mail, anything related—intellectually or socially—to homosexuality.

Queer people of color were also making zines in that era before *Dr. Smith* and *J.D.s*: people like Vaginal Davis—she was making zines in the '70s in LA, sort of tying into the punk scene—and of course because it was LA it was also about glamour and gossip. Then you had Latino folks creating things like *Homeboy Beautiful*, which came out in the late '70s and was recently republished.

Scott Treleaven: I was in film school in 1992 and then I decided to drop and move to London, England to kind of sort myself out, and actually go through the process of coming out. Because at that time I didn't think I was gay; nothing in the gay mainstream actually spoke to me or made any kind of sense to me whatsoever. So when I was in London, I became acquainted with Thee Temple of Psychick Youth, I got to spend the day with Derek Jarman, and I got turned on to these elements within the queer scene that were intensely political and had an entirely different personality to them that really resonated with me. So when I moved back to Canada I went looking for something that had that kind of gravity, that kind of sincerity. That's when I discovered zines. And the zines all had this sort of open but codified language: they talked about homocore and queercore and queer punk. For me, this fusion of sexuality with political awareness was extremely potent. I was, like, twenty years old. And in 1992, this was like stumbling through a doorway into an entirely new world. I couldn't just go online and Google *gay-comma-punk-comma-my hometown* and weed through the results. So finding things like zines, suggesting that there's this other world out there, it was kind of a lifechanging moment for me.

Brontez Purnell: It's like, the collective is never going to speak to you, so you always have to take entertainment into your own hands. You always have to be in control of your own voice because if you let other people control it, they're going to get very crucial things wrong.

Deke Nihilson: There was no internet to turn to. There weren't alternative sources of media, y'know—you had Dan Rather or your local daily capitalist newspaper and they were all saying the very same thing. The media blockade in the '80s was intense. The only alternative media at the time, at least in the Midwest, were fundamentalist Christian radio stations. Those people had spent fifty years having bingo games to raise the capital to buy AM transmitters in the middle of nowhere so that they could shriek about *Jeeesus!* Now we have a lot more media resources—the internet changed everything. Back then we didn't have that. But we had our photocopiers, so we did what we could with what we had.

DR. SMITH

Bruce LaBruce: For me, queercore started with Candy and her fanzine *Dr. Smith*. I wrote an article recently for AA Bronson's second collection of queer zines and I attributed everything to Dr. Smith—the character from *Lost in Space* and then

Dr. Smith no. 3

Candy's fanzine. Dr. Smith was this incredibly complex, hilarious—and stereotypically gay—kind of character, but he was everything that you'd ever want to be as homosexual; he was pompous, theatrical, sarcastic, devious conniving and criminal, but also a resourceful, witty, and imperious dandy. And he was a huge influence on me. He's a good example of a character who just doesn't fit in anywhere. He's totally selfish and self-absorbed, and incredibly entertaining. And Candy was probably the smartest and the best artist of any of us. She and G.B. and Caroline from Fifth Column had a long and tumultuous relationship well before I made the scene. Caroline and Candy had gone to high school together. I lived with all of them over the years. It was magical, until it wasn't.

J.D.s

G.B. Jones: Toronto is an experimental city, run by people who are probably involved with the Bilderberg Group, who have decided to eradicate history—to constantly build new, disposable buildings that people form no attachment to, so that their only attachments are to what they find through consumerism. I think it's an experiment that various corporations have come together to try on the people of Toronto. So, being bereft of history in Toronto, it's easy to conceptualize new

Punks at Togethers Bar, (gone now), a gay bar in Toronto

Punks at the Oranien Bar, a late-night gay bar in Kreuzberg

photo: Damien Blackinght

J.D.s no. 2

things. It leaves the field wide open, since there's no past. You have to look really hard to find a past in Toronto. And, actually, I *did*, and it was a major influence on *J.D.s*—finding the *Tattler*, those old magazines. I thought, *Wow—look what's been here before, I never knew about this.*

When you discover something like that, it's like this subversive element creeping in. Everyone always says, *Toronto's so clean.* It's been *wiped* clean. Like a brainwashing; all memories have been eradicated. So to find this message from the past, about the lives people had led, was just so influential and subversive that I thought, *I have to find a way to continue that.* So that in the future, once the history of *J.D.s* has been wiped clean from Toronto, someone will find this old zine in an old bookstore somewhere—although they're probably trying to wipe out the bookstores; they'll go to the Archives and find it there, and think, *Wow, look what used to happen here!* And hopefully be inspired.

Bruce LaBruce: It just seemed like we filled a niche that needed to be filled—there were a lot of queer punks. We talked a lot about how the roots of punk were very queer. It was all about exploring different political, social, sexual configurations—a lot of experimentation. Everyone from Phranc and Nervous Gender to Jayne County . . . Patti Smith . . . so it was just getting to the back to the roots of the original punk.

Adam Rathe: *J.D.s* is smart, it's funny, it's irreverent, it's weird, it's sexy, it's punk, and it has the *Anonymous Boy* cartoons, which are fantastic.

Jena von Brucker: I think there was something Warholian about the whole thing—putting somebody on the cover and crowning them prince of the homosexuals, sort of turning people into stars. There was a community around *J.D.s* because they put their friends in the things that they were doing.

Tony Arena: I was especially taken with the drawings by G.B. Jones, the Tom Girl drawings that were based on Tom of Finland. I'd never seen Tom of Finland, but I was really drawn to these Tom Girl pictures, and I wanted to draw something similar. So I drew what became the first Anonymous Boy drawing and sent it to the zine anonymously. And they got called Anonymous Boy drawings because G.B.—I'd written to her, like, *Don't say my name*, or whatever; I was still just a kid in the closet, basically. So she published this drawing in *J.D.s* from an Anonymous Boy, and I thought, *That's a really great name. It's like a cool punk rock name. I think*

J.D.s no. 1

from now on I'm going to call myself Anonymous Boy. And it became my name, at least in that little queer corner of the world. I'd been really into the punk rock scene, I'd been in punk bands by this point, but I had not yet integrated my secret queer self with my punk rock self. Getting involved in *J.D.s* gave me more courage than I'd ever had before.

The *Anonymous Boy* collections were basically drawings of queer punk boys in love, having sex and stuff like that. So I started to send them out, and I got all this mail back. All these kids were writing to me and saying that they loved it. I say kids, but actually I had to be careful about who I was sending it to, because some of the stuff was pretty explicit, X-rated. I mean, they were drawings, but they still could be considered dangerous—I'd already heard about Mike Diana, who'd been put in prison for doing comics in Florida and ordered not to draw anymore. So I had to be careful—I didn't want to go to fucking prison for drawing pictures. Anyway, people would write back and say how much they loved the zines, and that's when I started to realize that a whole new thing was happening, a queercore movement that wasn't just *J.D.s* anymore. *J.D.s* had inspired all these other zines, and it was actually starting to become a movement.

G.B. Jones: It was always a musical genre, from the beginning. We had been performing and I had met the women from Anti-Scrunti Faction, from Boulder, Colorado; they'd come up to Toronto and we'd started filming the Yo-Yo Gang. Through *J.D.s* I had also met Donna Dresch, and Laura Sister Nobody, and they were both in bands—Laura was in Snakepit, and Donna was in Dangermouse. Deke, who did *Homocore* magazine, had a band called Comrades in Arms . . . there were early queercore bands, people just weren't on record labels at that point. We were putting out our own records on our own labels, other people were putting out cassettes—the whole thing about being on a trendy label hadn't started yet.

Kathleen Hanna: Donna Dresch lived in Olympia, she was good friends with Tobi Vail, and she was on the cover of *Homocore*. She was kind of the gateway drug for us reading all this material, and there would be no Bikini Kill without *J.D.s* and *Homocore* and G.B. Jones. I would have no career without *Homocore*; I really wouldn't. I don't think I would have had the courage to make my own zine.

BIMBOX

Dennis Cooper: Johnny and Rex Boy sent me the first *Bimbox*—I think they just liked my books or something and sent it to me. I was super excited by what they were doing, and we became really good friends. I still think he was the great genius of the whole thing. What he was doing with *Bimbox* and *Double Bill*, those years when Johnny was completely on fire—it was incredibly brilliant. I think he was the great artist of that group. And the politics were so incredibly

Bimbox no. 2

wild, and unbelievably daring and fearless, and so creative and smart. I always felt like Johnny was the real god of that scene for me.

Johnny Noxzema: *Bimbox* was regularly seized at the border. Which is strange, because—certainly the issue with the pop-up dick and things like that, to source that material we would use old vintage magazines, and a lot of the images that I used were actually obtained in the US. In New York City there was a used bookstore called Gay Treasures that had old Tom of Finland chapbooks, *Physique Pictorial* magazines, and things like that. I'd buy them, take them home, cut them up and paste them in the zine. So vintage pornography that was purchased *legally* in New York City—if you take it *out* of the country, photocopy it, and try to mail it back into the US, it gets seized.

I found it very amusing that people were so worked up over something that was *photocopied*. That was just an invitation to press more buttons. The further we went, it was like, *They freaked out over that?* So, y'know, we would freak them out even more. For me it was influenced by *Weekly World News* more than anything. We found *Weekly World News* very hilarious. So a lot of it was based on things that were going on in *Weekly World News*.

Dennis Cooper: Johnny Noxzema would just say all this really outrageous stuff—he would take stances that were antiqueer, he would completely fuck with *everybody*, just to make everybody question everything. There was no status quo and there was no hierarchy, he didn't want anything to get *comfortable*. So he would attack *everybody*. He was vehemently against Burroughs, for instance. He was unbelievably negative about Burroughs, who, of course, was a big icon of queer punk. He was incredibly clever at pushing people's buttons and just saying the wrong thing in the right way and getting everybody quite in a tizzy. At the same time, people always

Bimbox no. 2

respected him and there were never, like, people trying to exile him. It was super interesting what he did.

Johnny Noxzema: We said ridiculous things, but it was really no different from what the Christian Right says about gay people—like, *All lesbians are into witchcraft*, or whatever. We would claim that there were experimental lesbian breeding centers so that we could reproduce without the help of men and things like that.

Sarah Schulman: I remember Gloria Berlin—that's G.B. Jones—and Jena and Johnny Noxzema came over to my apartment, at the height of AIDS crisis. Vito Russo, who was a very beloved figure in the queer community, was dying of AIDS, and I remember Johnny saying, *Vito Russo, what a nightmare!* So that was their position—they were very oppositional.

Johnny Noxzema: Vito Russo dismissed the works of John Waters as not being part of gay film! It's like, *Are you insane? John Waters is our best asset. How can you say that John Waters and Divine and all those movies aren't gay films?* I said something really horrible in the magazine—that we would dig him up and put a stake through his heart, that sort of thing.

Honestly, I wasn't into the punk scene that much. When I was in high school I loved X-Ray Spex and Nina Hagen and stuff like that—but honestly, I'd rather listen to Eartha Kitt than punk rock music at any given time. *Bimbox* had Peggy Lee concert reviews; we had a great tribute to Loretta Lynn at one point, a big tribute to Sylvester when he passed away. Ann-Margret was pretty popular in the magazine as well. I guess if *those* are considered punk, then it was punk . . . but I've always been very selective about the sort of music I like. Of course, I really loved Fifth Column, Glen Meadmore, Bratmobile . . . the Nancy Sinatras were fabulous. I'd consider them all to be queercore.

DOUBLE BILL

Eileen Myles: The Nova convention happened in 1979, and I was invited to be in it and maybe this lesbian novelist Jane Delynn was too; I can't remember how we both got to be there, but she had the idea to get a theatrical gun. We walked out on stage together, and she said to me, *C'mon, do your William Tell routine!*, and I put the apple on my head and she shot me, and I fell to the floor. And the room went really fucking silent. Because of all the things you weren't supposed to say about William S.

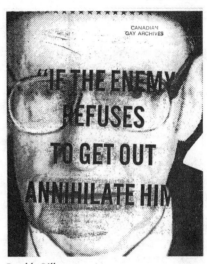

Double Bill no. 2

Burroughs at the Nova Convention—you weren't supposed to mention the small fact that he *killed his wife, in front of his child*. Y'know? But how, as women, could we forget that *that's what Burroughs did*?

Her death—like, she was the fertilizer or whatever that grew this incredible tree that is Burroughs's brain. Which may be true, or may be part of the truth, but it was still a monstrous act. When we walked backstage afterward nobody would look at us or talk to us. I think it's a part of punkness, that female desire to say what's in the room that is violating us. And it seemed like only two dykes . . . in the same way that Valerie Solanas was at least some kind of response to the whole world of Andy Warhol, whether it's right or wrong that she shot him. It was an important commentary that has never been celebrated; but somehow Burroughs's crime was a *spiritual act*. And we had to say, *That ain't so.*

Jena von Brucker: There was a lot of women-hating that went on in the gay community. And William Burroughs became a representation of that. He was idolized not just by gay men but by a lot of people in general—absolutely worshiped. And he shot his wife! I don't know, it seemed to be just a blip on the radar. It's like, *He shot his wife*—why are we just forgetting about that incident? Because he was some brilliant writer? We were kind of outraged by that.

Penny Arcade: William was also very homophobic. All those guys were homophobic, in a real sense. I mean, Allen Ginsberg actually said to me, while I was in Jack Smith's hospital room—while Jack was dying—Allen said to me, *I really haven't known that many people with AIDS.* He knew Howard Brookner, who made the film on Burroughs. And I looked at him and I said, *Allen, you're the most famous homosexual in the world. Howard is the only person you know who died of AIDS?* Because they had that masculine image, their hallmark of *real masculinity*.

Jena von Brucker: William Conrad played this loveable, plump, charming detective on TV. And we had this idea, putting the two of them next to each other. William Burroughs is terrible, and William Conrad is fantastic; the juxtaposition was hilarious to us. We put together our first issue in one night, sent it out, and people loved it.

G.B. Jones: After *J.D.s*, me, Caroline Azar, Jena von Brucker, Johnny Noxzema, and Rex did *Double Bill*. And that was much more fun to do because there were five of us. Each person did their own thing, we brought it all together, and we spent hours just *laughing* at what we had done.

Jena Von Brucker: I think the group of us working on *Double Bill* felt extremely alienated, even from the subculture that we existed in, and that made it easier to say things like that. So we made a lot of strong statements, we stayed up very late, and we drank a lot during those years—and I think all of that helped to fuel it.

Kathleen Hannah: We were inspired by *J.D.s*, *Homocore*, and especially by *Double Bill* by G.B. Jones, which changed my life. I could be a feminist and have a fucking sense of humor. I could talk about rape with a

Double Bill no. 2

weird fucked-up smile on my face, you know what I mean? Because it's my prerogative to do that. I went to a college where everybody read William S. Burroughs and had, like, William Burroughs books in their back pockets. And, y'know, he shot his fucking wife and got away with it, and G.B. Jones wasn't taking that shit. She was totally making fun of him. I felt so relieved, like I was the only person who was like, *Am I on crazy pills?* I'm not saying he wasn't a good writer, but I think we were trying to unmask the illusion of the rock star or the addicted writer. We were about creating community; we weren't about rock stars or individual fuckups who made this "great art" because they were wasted—this Jim Morrison myth that permeates our culture and is such bullshit.

Deke Nihilson: Sure, there was the whole thing with his wife, and some people raised a sustained critique of him as a misogynist. I think that kind of critique takes him way too literally. I don't think the point of his books was ever to run down women; he was simply interested in gay male space and culture. It's a version of the same thing as radical lesbian separatism, which does *not* equal man-hating. He was also really old-school—he was born in, what, the 1920s? To the family that inherited the fortune from the invention of the adding machine. So he did have sort of an upper-class frame of reference, a bit like Aleister Crowley; but he was something of a class traitor. He took the privileges that he came from and did these radical social things with them, and some of it was entirely solipsistic and self-referential. I mean, that's what *Junk* is, right? But he also sustained a critique of control systems and posited a means of resistance to them in ways that were pioneering. If you're going to judge an artist by their personal flaws, then there's not much art worth looking at; but art, when it's good, transcends even the sins of its creator. So . . . he remains a literary hero of mine, no matter what people's critiques of him are as a person.

Scott Treleaven: I mean, Burroughs was a *huge* influence on me. Massive. But part of G.B.'s brilliance is her contrarian nature. And taking these sacred homo icons and tearing them down is definitely a part of her MO.

HOMOCORE

Deke Nihilson: I was part of this midwestern punk rock scene that was remarkably tolerant of my homosexuality. I was out of the closet, but almost nobody else there was, and it was very isolating, even with friends—it wasn't like I had much of a love life or anything. Then I went up to Toronto for this Continental Anarchist Gathering, and I remember, within the first couple days they had a queer anarchist circle. And a bunch of people got together, sort of checking in with each other— everybody wanted scene reports, if you will: *What's going on in your town? What are people doing, what do people care about?*, and so on. These are people from New York and San Francisco, and Toronto, probably Chicago, places that had big scenes with enough queers in them that there was queer stuff going on. Well, I was from a place where I was pretty much *it*, and when my turn came, I said something like, *I'm the only person in my scene that's willing to be out as queer. I do what I can, but I feel like even just existing there is kind of a lot.*

The vibe I got from some people was kind of like, *That's too bad; you should move away or something,* but anyway . . . what's going on in New York? But Tom Jennings heard me. He was one person out of the crowd who thought, *Yeah, y'know, what about all those isolated kids out there? How can we break that?*

Tom Jennings: It started with the anarchist bookstore crowd. We went to this anarchist conference in Toronto, and I didn't really know anybody. When we got there, I met Deke, who lived in Kansas City, and was thinking about moving to San Francisco. When I came back from the anarchist conference, I did the first issue of *Homocore*, with Burroughs on the cover. It was sort of done in response to my experience in Toronto, where I met Deke and Bruce. The straight boys were throwing rocks and getting righteous. We were all hanging out, like, *Oh, Queer punks, cool!*

Homocore no. 5

Deke Nihilson: For me, *Homocore* started with data entry. We had all these letters and Tom was like, *sit, type.* I'm like, *Can we just write this out by hand?* Because that's how I did my zine. And he's like, *No, type!* I didn't even know how to type at that time. As I started writing pieces for *Homocore* and coordinating other volunteers I slowly (or not so slowly) became as involved in making it happen as he did. I think Tom burned out on the zine. He was ready to stop doing it, but I was like, *No, the kids need it—we have to do this!* So then I pretty much helmed one or two issues worth of editorship. I don't think I was ever formally a coeditor, but I was committed to it. Not just because he put me on the *cover* of no. 5, although he did that. He didn't tell that he was going to do that first—I was shocked, I was like, *Oh my god, that's me, I'm a star!*—five copies for my mother, y'know, that whole thing. But yeah, it got huge. He'd been doing it on 8 ½ × 11 paper, folded and stapled, and by the fourth issue or so he was doing it on newsprint because we were selling so many thousands of copies.

Larry Livermore: I'd already known Tom for a year or two, from the punk scene. He was part of a collective called Shred of Dignity, a skate collective, and there were a bunch of cool people living at their warehouse. They did me a big favor when I was starting Lookout! Records, letting me keep the answering machine in their warehouse. I lived up in the mountains where they had no phone, so my official office was an answering machine sitting on a fridge at the Shred of Dignity warehouse. And that's kind of how I got to know Tom. I can't remember exactly

what year *Homocore* came into being, but it was something that was
being talked about for a while. I know Tom expressed a lot of discontent
over how he felt marginalized at 924 Gilman, even though Gilman was a
very opening and welcoming place. It just felt like there was something
missing. And I agreed with him, because early on in the punk scene,
back in the '70s, it wasn't like the sexuality was a big issue. That was
the whole point: it wasn't an issue at all. There were all sorts of gay
people all over the place and you didn't even think about it—it was San
Francisco, and it was kind of integrated in every way.

But a few years on, when that scene had died away and Gilman
came into being, the crowd was younger and fresher but also much
whiter and straighter. In fact, almost completely straight, at least on
the surface. You would look at it and say, *This is really wholesome, really
suburban.* And that's what it kind of felt like. We needed to sort of open
things up again. We did a show at the Deaf Club in the Mission, which
was a venue during the very early punk scene that had kind of gone
away—it was a club for deaf people, and they let people put on punk
shows there because the noise didn't bother them—and they'd dance
to the vibrations and the stomping on the floor. So for the first time in
a few years we did a show there, a *Homocore* benefit with MDC, and I
can't remember who else played. Basically I was just hanging around
with Tom and sharing his passion for opening up the scene and exposing
people to some things that they might not have heard.

Mykel Board: *Homocore* was brilliant, and it brought a lot of people out.
Because until that time, people felt trapped; they felt like, *Well, OK, I like
guys; does that mean I have to like disco? They all go together, right? Those
horrible clothes and disco music?* So if I like guys I have to like disco and
have bad taste in clothes. *Homocore*, Tom's magazine, and the stuff that
Bruce LaBruce was doing, freed people from that—I can like guys and
have a black leather jacket. It was like a great leap forward, and it liberated a lot of people who'd been kept in the closet because they liked stuff
that wasn't gay. What could they do? They had to choose! *Homocore* told
them, *You don't have to choose; you can have your cock and eat it too.*

Deke Nihilson: By the time we stopped there were not dozens but hundreds of queercore zines. When it started there were a handful. By the
time we finished doing *Homocore*, hundreds of people were showing up

to gatherings like SPEW and SPEW 2—I think there was a 3 too. So we kind of felt like, *mission accomplished.*

Tom Jennings: At some point, we started to find older zines that were interesting. There were magazines like the *18 Wheeler*, which was truck drivers that wanted to get or give blowjobs and have sex at truck stops. It was typewritten and mimeographed—this was in the late '60s or early '70s. There was *Fag Rag*, which was hippie-esque; not quite like *Homocore*, but it served a similar purpose, it was arty, it was aesthetic—whereas the *18 Wheeler* was, *Wanna give a blowjob? Here's my phone number and my route through New York and New Jersey. Let's get down to business. Fag Rag* was more, like, impenetrable poetry. We'd get so much poetry sent to *Homocore*. God, I hate poetry. But we published it.

Well, we didn't publish it; actually, we published issue 5 1/2 to get rid of all the poetry. We would get all this poetry and didn't know what to do with it. People, y'know—most of it was really, really heartfelt stuff, and it was really important to them. And you pour out your heart on a piece of paper, but it doesn't mean anyone else is necessarily going to *get* it. So as editor, you have to decide. We'd adopted this policy fairly early on, Deke and I, that we'd publish everything that was sent to us that was coherent and not hateful. Well, even some hateful stuff. We published some hateful stuff because it was funny, in our context. So we published every goddamn thing that was sent to us. But the poetry just built up and we felt really guilty, so we did a poetry issue between issues 5 and 6. No one ever wanted it . . . but we did publish everything that was ever sent to us, so I don't feel guilty anymore.

Toward the end, when we published *Homocore* no. 7, Deke and I were just burned out with all these kids writing in, like, *My mother found out I was gay, they sent me to this prison school, and you're my last hope* . . . God, we wrote everybody back, but it just became too much. And then—it's interesting, as zine culture kind of crested for me, in '91, '92, the internet started picking up.

MAXIMUM ROCKNROLL

Mykel Board: *Maximum Rocknroll* magazine was started in the '80s in California by Tim Yohannan, and it was, like, the punk rock bible. They had reviews of the punk rock shows, they introduced the world to punk rock; it was at one time the largest circulation punk rock magazine of any in the world. Everybody knew *Maximum Rocknroll,* everybody learned about the new records, and the new bands, and knew what was happening from *Maximum Rocknroll.*

They had strong politics, which I often disagreed with—that's how I began to write for them. They were very . . . hardcore. They were very totalitarian; something could be punk rock, but if it was what they considered sexist, racist, homophobic, or whatever, they wouldn't talk about it, they wouldn't print it, they wouldn't introduce the music. It had to agree with them. I read an interview with Tim Yohannan in another magazine, a fanzine called *Ripper*—I read this interview, and I wrote to the fanzine and said, *This guy is an asshole!* The idea of punk is to celebrate all different kinds, all kinds of music, *everybody* who's acting on the outside. Later I met Tim Yohannan, when I went to California. We became friends, and he asked me if I wanted to write for *Maximum Rocknroll.* I said, *Yeah, I'll write if you print anything I write,* and he agreed. So I've been writing, up until his death—and I've still been writing, but since his death my columns have been occasionally censored. Tim would never do it, but the new editors have.

Tom Jennings: *Maximum Rocknroll,* pain in the ass as Tim Yohannan was . . . I really liked Tim Yohannan, but we had screaming arguments. He was—I didn't personally experience this, but I was told that he was sort of this raging homophobe, the classic Leninist-communist type that thought that homosexuality was a bourgeois indulgence that would go away. He never said that to me. So I don't know whether people just have chips on their shoulders and are reading into his behavior or they heard something. But anyways, we got along fine . . . except when we didn't get along, which was most of the time. But a lot of people loved him dearly. And I did, too. He was a major factor in punk and a major force in San Francisco.

Maximum Rocknroll was sort of a working-class version of punk that was literate and smart without the academic, privileged view. It was people in the trenches, people writing letters. The letters column in *Maximum Rocknroll* was a fucking goldmine. And that's how *Homocore* really started, as far as I'm concerned. The letters are just fascinating. Homophobe or not, Tim Yohannan enabled a lot of queer punk through his willingness to just let speech be speech. A lot of queer people wrote in; it was one of those things where someone writes something positive and there's a cascade of *me toos*. And then there's, like, *Fuck you, faggots!*, and all the other usual responses. I wrote some polemic thing, and I think Deke did as well. That might have been where I initially met Deke, was in the letters column. I wrote a fairly—to me—major letter that got published in *Maximum Rocknroll*, that got a lot of responses, and that was certainly a factor in starting *Homocore*.

Brontez Purnell: I had friends gave me the queer issue of *Maximum Rocknroll* from 1992—but this was probably 1997 when I got it. There was Vaginal Cream Davis, Bruce LaBruce. Vaginal Cream Davis was in a cop outfit and Bruce was on his back getting fucked. There was lots of stuff. I think Tribe 8 was in it. Bikini Kill was in it, blah blah blah. I thought there was no one else in the world like me . . . then I was like: there are lots of other people like me.

12

WHY DON'T YOU JUST GET TOGETHER?

THE SPEW CONVENTION AND HOMOCORE CHICAGO (1992–2001)

Larry-Bob Roberts: There were several events that ended up being called SPEW. The first SPEW was in Chicago in 1991, organized by Steve LaFreniere. There was a daylong zine fest; people would do readings, and drag performances, and I think there were some film projections as well; there was a show with Fifth Column and Vaginal Davis . . . so that was the first SPEW.

Mark Freitas: It was one of those moments of convergence. You hear about that show the Sex Pistols did where everyone in the audience formed a band—or the

Larry-Bob Roberts. Photo by Mark Freitas

Velvet Underground album, everyone who bought that album started a band—that's like what came out of SPEW. It kind of sent the scene into hyperdrive.

Joanna Brown: The hundred people who knew about queer zines were all in the same room for once. I met Ms. Davis; I met the performance artist Larry Seger (who has since passed away), I met Suzie Silver—I met all these people. And then that night Fifth Column played, and Laura Sister Nobody played—I had gone home in between the zine conference

LA'S BABYLONIAN TEENAGE LOVE GARGANTUESS
VAGINAL CREME DAVIS

TORONTO'S EXPLODING DYKE-CORE INEVITABLE
FIFTH COLUMN

KNEEDEEPDISH HOUSE BY THING MAGAZINE'S
**ROBERT FORD & TEE ADKINS
W/DJ BURLE AVANT ★ MC LIZ**

Saturday May 25th 10 pm 6 Bucks Please
Hot House   1569 N Milwaukee Avenue   Chicago

SHOWTHEFUCKUPMISSMISSY

Early SPEW flyers

and the show and read her zine, *Sister Nobody*, so I went up to her after the show, and I was like, *Your zine really affected me*. We talked for a while, and she introduced me to Donna Dresch. Then a few months later I wrote to Donna, I sent her some money for her zine *Chainsaw* and I said, *Hey, do you remember meeting me?* She writes back, *I'm in Fifth Column now and we're coming to Chicago. Do you know where we can play?*

So I called Steve Lafreniere, because I knew he was the guy to talk to. And he goes, this guy Mark keeps bugging me too, the two of you want to do the same thing so why don't you just get together?

Mark Freitas: Joanna and I were both friends with G.B. Jones—I had been in a movie that she had done, she and I were pen pals—and her band Fifth Column wanted to play a show in Chicago. And we were like, *Hell yeah. Let's use it as a way to launch Homocore Chicago*. And it was huge! There was already a bit of a scene in Chicago around that kind of queer/punk/industrial dynamic, and coming out of SPEW . . .

Joanna Brown: Riot grrrl was starting to hit right around the same time—

Mark Freitas: —and Joan Jett Blakk was running for president, people were going to Joan Jett Blakk benefits, and a lot of that crowd was very "alternative" . . .

Early Homocore flyer

Larry-Bob at Homocore Chicago. Photo by Mark Freitas

Joan Jett Blakk at Homocore Chicago. Photo by Mark Freitas

Bruce LaBruce and Klaus von Brucker at Homocore Chicago. Photo by Mark Freitas

Deke Nihilson at Homocore Chicago. Photo by Mark Freitas

Steve Lafreniere at Homocore Chicago. Photo by Mark Freitas

Joanna Brown: So we made posters—we became the king and queen of postering—and we'd make quarter-sheet flyers. If I walked out my door I'd have twenty of them in my back pocket, and anyone who looked like they'd be even vaguely interested, I would hand them a flyer.

Mark Freitas: I took the word *Homocore* from the masthead of the magazine and blew it up on the xerox machine until it turned into a nice big logo—the idea being that you could see it from about a block away. And the brand kind of became bigger than the bands—because a lot of our crowd wanted queer punk but they didn't necessarily know the bands.

Joanna Brown: The Czar Bar was an old-man bar. Nelson Algren used to hang out there. It went back to the '30s. We were bringing in huge crowds. People realized you didn't have to be twenty-one, and we were having great bands . . .

Homocore Chicago. Photo by Mark Freitas

Mark Freitas: You *did* have to be twenty-one—we just didn't care.

Joanna Brown: Chester, the owner, loved it because he was selling shitloads of beer. His bartenders were making tons of tips.

Mark Freitas: But his first reaction—

Joanna Brown: —his first reaction, he saw two boys kissing in the back and he was like, *I don't know if I like this . . .* And we were like, *Chester, how much money did you make tonight?* And he goes, *Oh . . . never mind.*

Homocore Chicago. Photo by David Rustile

Mark Freitas: Eventually they brought in a promoter who wanted to take over the door and the sound; and there were also issues with us wanting to do more all-ages shows. Generally it was cool that the younger kids that were under twenty-one could sneak in and pass under the radar. The one time that really became an issue was when Los Crudos played.

Martín Sorrondeguy: I remember the first time Mark called me to play Homocore. And I had gone to Homocore shows, I went and saw Vaginal Davis and some other stuff. So Mark was like, *Now, we love Los Crudos, and . . . I know nobody in the band is queer, but we were wondering if you would come and play a show at Czar Bar.* I said, *How do you know nobody from Crudos is queer?* He was like, *Oh! . . .* There was this silence, and he was like, *Is there something I don't know?* And I was like, *I* think *so! . . .* Assuming that I wasn't queer, it was nice that they invited us to come play, I thought that was awesome. Our bigger issue was playing a bar.

Mark Freitas: Crudos' fans were really young—there were fifteen-, sixteen-year-old kids—

Joanna Brown: They were Latino, and they got carded.

Mark Freitas: They were refused entry. And the band was upset, understandably. But that led to us going, *Let's find an all-ages space.*

Joanna Brown: When we decided to leave the Czar Bar—almost that *night* we started getting calls from all these major bars, courting us. But we said, *Nope, it's gotta be all-ages.* So we moved, mostly, to the Fireside Bowl. Bikini Kill came through, Sleater-Kinney came through . . .

Mark Freitas: God Is My Co-Pilot, which at the time was a big No Wave band, Scissor Girls, Team Dresch, Huggy Bear's first show in Chicago was with us . . . When we came into the scene, the perception was that punk was this macho, homophobic thing. We kind of reclaimed it and made a space for people that had been squeezed out of the scene. And once that space was there, it didn't go away. Then bands like Le Tigre and Sleater-Kinney really exploded. And we didn't need to be there; they would book at the Metro, with mostly queer crowds of hundreds if not thousands. Did we need to be involved? No. Our last show was with Le Tigre—I think Bride of No-No opened.

Joanna Brown: We decided to just close it out right. To tie it back to that night when Mark and I met at the Bikini Kill show—when Bikini Kill played Czar Bar, there were forty or fifty people there. I remember I got there early—I had written to Kathleen Hanna for a copy of *Bikini*

Kill zine, and I think I owed her two dollars or something. So I went up and introduced myself and I said, *Y'know, I'm putting together a Fifth Column show here*. And she was *so* encouraging. So to go from having that moment with her to her closing out this thing—Homocore Chicago—that was such a big part of my life, was perfect.

Chris Wilde: Chicago was the inspiration for Homocore Minneapolis. We'd take road trips to go to Homocore Chicago shows, and people eventually caught on that there was enough support in the Twin Cities. I mean, Minneapolis is huge for independent music, and there was a whole network of basement shows and DIY spaces. The Homocore Minneapolis scene was a little later in coming. It started more in the mid-1990s and hit its peak in the late '90s. Ed Varga was one of the main people to kickstart Homocore Minneapolis.

Larry-Bob Roberts: Homocore Minneapolis was similar to Homocore Chicago. They provided places where touring queer bands could play. There was actually a *Homocore Minneapolis: Live and Loud* compilation that Homocore Minneapolis put out. Ed Varga was involved, and then Ed moved to Olympia and eventually started the Homo A Gogo festivals in the Northwest.

Ed Varga: I discovered music before I discovered anything about being queer. I grew up in a small town in Wisconsin, Chippewa Falls, in the '80s, and being queer just wasn't an option. Also I'm trans, and nobody talked about that, there was no space to be that. So I feel like punk rock saved my life, growing up in a small town as a freak. If anything, I could always identify as just being one of the freaks. When I saw that there were bands playing queer punk rock, my mind just exploded. It always felt like I had to make a compromise, where if I wanted to have a sense of community, or find a date, I had to go to these clubs. With queercore it was like—I don't have to make these compromises anymore.

In Minneapolis in the '90s, Extreme Noise was a big part of the scene, and it was not very female-friendly. It was not women-fronted, it was very macho, it was pretty homophobic—it just wasn't where I wanted to be, it wasn't a cool scene to be a part of. So trying to carve out a niche that wasn't about that was important to me.

13

BASEBALL BATS AND HIGH-HEEL SHOES
PUNKS ON PARADE
(SAN FRANCISCO 1989/CHICAGO 1993)

Deke Nihilson: We were punks—we were intentionally planting ourselves outside mainstream culture. That community that had grown around Homocore and Klubstitute and the seeds of the queercore scene in San Francisco did a float in the Gay Pride Parade in 1989 in San Francisco. This rich benefactor rented a junk car and a tow truck, and we painted the car to look like a police car. Somebody, probably the Klubstitute guys, made a giant papier-mâché high-heel, which we stuck into the back of the car as if was crushing the police car. And then we had a couple bags of high-heel shoes that we handed out to the crowd so they could do their own pounding on the car. And we towed this thing down Market Street as our parade entry—just let it all hang out that we were the punks, and we hated the police because they hated us.

Silas Howard: Harry Dodge and I were like nineteen years old when we moved to San Francisco. We didn't have any community; we were hanging out with straight bike messengers, going to hear indie bands . . . And we went to the pride parade that year, and we saw them do that—Leslie, Donna Dresch, all these people were there. It was a crystalizing moment. We were like, *These are our people*. We had been with ACT UP, we had been political, but we hadn't yet found that. And it was like falling in love. It was like, *Oh,* there *you are.*

Justin Vivian Bond talks about that same moment too. They pulled up with the cop car and all moved around it, Leslie Mah and all these people who I would eventually get to know. I remember a bunch of punks pulling out baseball bats and proceeding to smash the cop car and I was like, *Yes!* I connected to that. And Justin Vivian is like, *I remember that moment too, but I remember there was this box of high-heel*

Homocore Chicago at the 1994 Chicago Pride Parade. Photo by Mark Freitas

Homocore Chicago 1994, photo by Mark Freitas

Homocore Chicago 1994, photo by Mark Freitas

shoes, and everyone just took out a shoe and started beating the car with high heel shoes.

Justin Vivian Bond: They had taken an apple crate, bolted it to the trunk of the car, and filled it with high heels. So I jumped into the parade, grabbed a high heel, and just started pounding on this police car. We basically destroyed this police car. And so all of these people became my friends. And then I had a community. It was a life-changing day.

Silas Howard: I love that we have these butch and femme memories— for me it was the baseball bats and for Justin it was the high-heel shoes.

Joanna Brown: The first year we were in the Pride Parade, we paid our money to get in, we were very polite, we went by all the rules.

Mark Freitas: We paid our money, but they didn't. They were supposed to give us armbands, a position in the parade and so on. They cashed our check but they didn't respond, didn't give us a position in the parade.

Joanna Brown: So we just made one up. We started passing out flyers, saying, *Hey, if you want to join us this is where we're going to be*. People brought pots and pans to bang on; I think Mark went out and bought a boombox that morning. And we had this huge banner we had painted the night before that said *Homocore Chicago—Proud of What?*

Mark Freitas: We were behind the WAC (Women's Action Coalition) drum corps, and they were getting mad at us because we weren't drumming in time—

Joanna Brown: And we were right in front of the Thousand Waves Health Spa karate group or whatever, and they actually went to the parade monitor and asked to have us removed from the parade because we were being *disruptive*. That was one of the proudest moments of my life. I loved the fact that someone wanted me removed from a fucking *parade* because I was too disruptive.

Mark Freitas: The thing that was kind of moving about it—when we first started out it was maybe twenty or thirty people, but by the time we got to the end of the route we had at least doubled in number. You would hear a piercing scream coming from one side of the street, and some punk girl from Milwaukee would come running and join in—and another, and another.

14

WE WERE SO READY
RIOT GRRRL EMERGES (EARLY 1990S)

Sarah Schulman: If you look at the very early all-women bands—Fanny, for example, which was the first all-women rock band, they'd play at the Fillmore East in the East Village, and there were a *lot* of dykes in that scene; and then there were people like Pat Place, and bands like Y Pants with Gail Vachon—Christine Vachon's sister—and Barbara Ess, who is a well-known artist, they would play toy instruments. There were women's underground music scenes that predate riot grrrl, people making work in the '70s, downtown.

RIOT GRRRL MANIFESTO

BECAUSE us girls crave records and books and fanzines that speak to US that WE feel included in and can understand in our own ways.

BECAUSE we wanna make it easier for girls to see/hear each other's work so that we can share strategies and criticize-applaud each other.

BECAUSE we must take over the means of production in order to create our own meanings.

BECAUSE viewing our work as being connected to our girlfriends-politics-real lives is essential if we are gonna figure out how what we are doing impacts, reflects, perpetuates, or DISRUPTS the status quo.

BECAUSE we recognize fantasies of Instant Macho Gun Revolution as impractical lies meant to keep us simply dreaming instead of becoming our dreams AND THUS seek to create revolution in our own lives every single day by envisioning and creating alternatives to the bullshit christian capitalist way of doing things.

BECAUSE we want and need to encourage and be encouraged in the face of all our own insecurities, in the face of beergutboyrock that tells us we can't play our instruments, in the face of "authorities" who say our bands/zines/etc are the worst in the US and

The "Riot Grrrl Manifesto"

Kathleen Hanna: I mean there were tons of great bands with women in them—the Avengers, X-Ray Spex, the Slits, ESG . . .

Kim Gordon: When I started there were a lot of women playing music. The Slits were around, The Raincoats, The Bags, The Avengers. I actually feel like I had a lot of women role models when I started. The no wave scene—Connie Burg from Mars, Lydia Lunch, Barbara Ess from The Static, Malaria! in Germany. It was actually a pretty rich time. But it seemed like in the '80s there were fewer women, really. I mean, there was Kim Deal and me; I was hard pressed to think of other women in bands. There was Teresa Nervosa from the Butthole Surfers and Yoshimi from the Boredoms . . . I'm sure there were others, but there didn't seem to be many.

Sara Marcus: Riot grrrl began in 1991 when members of the bands Bikini Kill and Bratmobile moved from Olympia, Washington, across the country to Washington, DC, for the summer, and they started

Lyric sheet to Bikini Kill's "Rebel Girl" taken from the "New Radio" 7"

making a weekly fanzine with their friend Jen Smith called *Riot Grrrl*. Then they decided to hold an all-girl meeting at the Positive Force house in Arlington, Virginia, to get to know other girls in the DC punk scene and talk about the status of punk rock and revolution—that was what the flyer said. And the meetings caught on. They went back to Olympia, meetings started in Olympia, meetings kept happening in DC—and as people moved, they started meetings in other places throughout the country. At the same time, these bands were touring—Bikini Kill especially—giving out zines, giving out flyers, spreading these ideas about girls and feminism and punk rock that were percolating around the scene in Olympia and DC.

The cultural space for young women to express frustration and anger wasn't being occupied, the cultural space for young women to speak out about all the stuff going in the political sphere was vacant; so riot grrrl came in, and as one person I interviewed for my book said, *We were so ready—it took almost nothing for us to jump in and start doing things, because it was exactly what we had been waiting for.*

Larry Livermore: Riot grrrl was kind of the women's liberation movement of the punk scene, and it served some of the same purposes. One of the reasons women's liberation started is that during the hippie, New Left period there was some real sexism going on. There was one leader who said, *The only position for women in the movement is prone*; another said, basically, *Keep the brown rice coming in.* And women, understandably, said, *That's bullshit. We're turning society upside down and we're going to have an equal part in it.* Riot grrrl expressed it in similar terms—like, *I'm not going to hold your leather jacket at the back of the pit anymore; I'm going to be in the pit. And I'm going to make a safe place for people my size and for all people of all sizes*—that whole attitude. I think riot grrrl and queercore kind of arose out of the same energy, even if they didn't always understand each other. But I think mostly they did. A lot was done cooperatively, in cooperation with each other.

Brontez Purnell: People thought riot grrrl was all bands, but riot grrrl was a collective of activists, dancers, painters. It's not just people making music. It's a holistic response to homophobia, racism, systemic oppression, a lot of things. It's the friend that lets you sleep on their couch when you can't pay your rent. It's a lot of things.

G.B. Jones: Queercore and riot grrrl were almost synonymous in the early '90s, for a certain period of time. And then as they started to get more media attention, the media tried to wipe out the queer in riot grrrl. The media got hold of it and twisted it around to the point where none of the original women who started riot grrrl would talk to the media anymore. As soon as I read that, I thought, *Yeah, I'm gonna stop talking to the media too! Why didn't I think of that years ago?* It's like, why hit yourself over the head with a brick, y'know?

Cookie: I think the media picked up, with riot grrrl, on these images of teenagers wearing baby-doll dresses, and combat boots, and a lot of girls who were white and conventionally attractive. That was easier than actually paying attention to their message or what they were trying to do, like fighting sexual violence. And it's interesting because I do think that in the early 1990s there was this moment when gay stuff became more mainstream. There was the famous *Vanity Fair* cover with of Cindy Crawford shaving K.D. Lang. It was this moment when lesbian-chic entered into the mainstream. But I don't think that extended to, like, dirty-punk-dykes, who were maybe fat or didn't shave . . . that wasn't as easy to swallow.

Sara Marcus: It is so much easier for capitalism to use a female body, that a man might want, to sell shit than it is to use queer people and queer bodies. Jack Halberstam has this whole riff, like, everything can be used for capitalism except the butch lesbian body. Riot grrrl just fits into an overall pattern: girls are interesting to the media. They don't get in the way of capitalism. Queer desire generally operates at the margins, which I think is awesome. I think that's a great position of liberation for queer art—except when you're being liberated from ever getting a decent wage for your creative product.

Hannah Blilie: It was frustrating and weird to have to explain feminism in such a basic way to people all the time. Like, *So you consider yourself a* feminist *band, huh? That's cute! Isn't* that *quaint?* Growing up in a sort of punk rock bubble, we didn't have to explain these things to people, we were already talking about feminism and politics on a way more radical level. And then to have to go through it over and over again . . . I remember people would ask Nathan all the time, *What's it like to be in a band with these crazy ladies?* And we were like, *Are you fucking* kidding *me? This is the year 2000-whatever. Yeah, we're women in a band. Yes, she's fat. What the fuck? It's not a big deal!* I think we felt a big responsibility, coming from where we did, to talk about these ideas all the time, but it was annoying how much I needed to explain. And just the bullshit of playing with these horrible sexist bands, being exposed to the mainstream rock world and the horrible sexist attitudes there, and really just feeling like the odd group out. We were kind of caught in between, because we were getting shit from the punk rock side for "selling out" and being successful, and then we were getting shit from these mainstreams folks who just didn't understand our message, our identity or where we were coming from.

Penny Arcade: I was performing *Bitch, Dyke, Faghag, Whore* in Boston in 1991 and Tinúviel, who was one of the early riot grrrls from Olympia, was on my crew. She was a young girl and she was very modest and almost didn't talk to me the whole time. Then the last day of the show she came up to me and handed me a bunch of zines and said, *We need you to come to Olympia, we need you to help lead the riot grrrl revolution.* And I was like, *OK, this sounds interesting* . . . I started to read the zines and I really flipped out. I loved the zines. I was like, *Oh my god, this is a feminism that I can identify with,* because I hated second-wave feminism. I thought they were elitist; they were against whores, against strippers. Their big problem was that they didn't want to be housewives. Like, look at all the fucking working poor. *My* mother was working seventy hours a week in a fucking sweatshop. She would have loved to be a housewife. I would have loved to have my mother at home, y'know. My mother worked all the time.

I just found second-wave feminism so elitist. And now here were these zines that were antihomophobic, antiracist, anticlassist—and feminist—and I was like, *Yes, I totally identify with this*. And I immediately got involved with the riot grrrl movement. But within like four months . . . Riot Grrrl New York formed and I would go to events, but it was immediately taken over as, like a, *cool* thing where everybody was *cool*. There would be people trying to read, young girls trying to read or play music— the place would be packed and there would be all these people talking and flirting and just ignoring what was happening on stage.

Lynn Breedlove: Lesbians were pissed at us. They were all like, you're stomping around on all this work we've done. You're wagging rubber dicks, getting blow jobs, talking about boinking, fisting—it was just wrong to them. Sex-radical dykes—it was the opposite of what they had been doing. And we would make fun of them, like, *Ha ha, Birkenstocks, tie-dye*, whatever. They were (rightfully) insulted, they were offended— we were insulting them, we were saying, *You're old, you're dumb*. But of course at the same time we totally admired everything that they'd done. We had read everything that they'd written, we had their books on our shelves, we studied very carefully everything that they had said and done.

And then we went on to build on that, to say that isn't working anymore and this isn't working anymore. We're going to take these things and create the next level. We're sex radicals. If you're saying that we're in charge of our bodies, if that's what feminism is all about, then great—I should be able to run around with my tits out, and say, *Stop looking at my tits. It's like, an elbow—a tit, what? It's my pecs, so what?* I should be able get a blow job, I should be able to fuck with a rubber dick, I should be able to do all that stuff because it's my body. I'm in charge, right? That's what you said, mom. It was totally like a child and their mom, y'know. You're hitting puberty, and you start fighting and start rebelling, and then the mom doesn't like it, and the kid is like, *You don't like it? Good, how about more of that! Ha, in your face!*

It took a while, probably fifteen or twenty years of us all doing a lot of discussing and trying to find the common ground—that we appreciated them and were just taking it to the next level, expressing it differently. And then they were like, *OK, you have our blessing.*

We always said we were riot hags, not riot grrrls—because the riot grrrls were a lot of younger, straight women, and we were old dykes. But we played together, we were talking the same language, talking about the same things. We had a lot in common—we were loud, we didn't know what we were doing, we were really rudimentary musicians with rudimentary equipment. I mean, there were some quite brilliant musicians in there—Jody Bleyle is a brilliant bass player, and Kaia is great guitar player, and Kathleen is a genius vocalist, obviously; there were many great singers and lyricists. I think mostly what we had in common was that a lot of our lyrics were about, *Hey, fuck you, we're pissed off. This is the new feminism. This is how we're doing it now—and if you don't like it, suck my dick.*

15

TEMPERS FLARE
TENSIONS IN TORONTO (LATE 1980S)

Adam Rathe: When you're passionate about stuff, tempers flare—especially when attention is starting to be paid. When you're in a band that people are starting to like, or making a zine that people are starting to read, or you're making films that people have started to pay attention to, there's jealously, there's spite, and there are egos and feelings.

Eileen Myles: In any community of writers you have fights. Especially at the point where people's careers are starting to take off—there's a lot of, *You're in; you're not in.* By the end of the '80s a lot of people who'd been friends were not friends any more. People didn't speak for ten years.

Dennis Cooper: The rivalry between Bruce and Johnny was intense.

Johnny Noxzema: *Me? Bruce?* No, no, no . . . I mean . . . well, we had our issues. I guess today it would be internet bullying—mutual bullying. But back then, things moved a lot more slowly.

Glenn Belverio: By the time I became friends with Bruce they were starting to have their falling-out. I started doing my fanzine called *Pussy Grazer*, which Bruce LaBruce was a contributor to. And then there was *Bimbox*, which was Johnny Noxzema and his psychiatrist husband.

Bruce LaBruce: *Bimbox* was published by a very strange duo—these two gay men, a one-legged psychiatrist and his kept boy. I called them Pegleg and Demented Chicken, because Noxzema had a rooster-like haircut. They were actually quite wealthy, and they were kind of posing as queer punks. And they took extremely radical polemical positions. They hated

PEOPLE

More Than in Your Face

Bad Boy Canadian 'Zine Editors Johnny Noxema and Rex Boy
Go Straight for the Jugular With *Bimbox*

BY ADAM BLOCK

The editors of the Canadian-based 'zine *Bimbox* wrote in their second issue, "Magazines like *The ADVOCATE* and *OutLook* have but one mandate: to systematically render the entire international lesbian and gay population brain-dead." With the release of their third issue, they'd sentenced all "breeders" to death, promising, "Everything that is heterosexual—from organized religion to Ziploc freezer bags—WILL be exterminated forever from the face of this planet." By the fourth issue they'd declared war on gay and lesbian culture, announcing, "Fact: ALL victims of gay bashing DESERVE what they get," and naming the entire staff of *The ADVOCATE* as among those who "should have their heads bashed in with lead pipes."

The provocateurs behind this Xeroxed outrage, editors Johnny Noxema, 23, and Rex Boy, 22, sport requisite Doc Martens, black T-shirts, jeans, and leather jackets with chains. At a meeting at San Francisco's posh Cliff House hotel, though, they prove soft-spoken, even polite.

"We're Canadian," Rex Boy offers almost apologetically. "It's a civil country. We started *Bimbox* for fun, but as it's progressed, it's become more of a forum for our political vision: an expression of anger."

"We still do it for fun," the wiry and kinetic Noxema grins, his eyes flashing. "You know I don't drive around in a pickup truck, hitting clones on the head with lead pipes, but the thought has certainly crossed my mind."

Noxema's immodest proposals have courted controversy, though. An anarchist bookstore refused to stock *Bimbox*. The New York–based 'zine *Pansy Grease* wrote, "We bash George Bush with golf clubs, not our brothers and sisters (whatever their

mainstream gay culture to be very bodybeautiful-oriented," he recalls. "I couldn't fit into that group and felt ostracized. People didn't think of me as a gay person; they thought of me as a geek."

Now a successful psychologist, Rex Boy earns enough to allow the seam the financial freedom to distribute their 'zine for free and to stay in quite civilized hotel suites along their recent transcontinental expedition.

Noxema grew up in a small East Canadian town with parents he calls "racist, homophobic monsters." He fled to Toronto as a teenager, only to find "no unity between the gay and lesbian communities. They were either disco clones or granola lesbians," he snarls. "They'd march together the last Sunday in June and then return to business as usual. I didn't relate at all."

Noxema and Rex Boy met in 1986 and soon moved in together. Two years later they released the first issue of their 'zine, mailing 100 free copies across Canada and the United States. They dubbed *Bimbox* "the magazine that subscribes to you."

That idea, along with the "slash-irreverence" content (the stock exposes "I Puted Pat Califia" and the cocksucking collagen quickly found an appreciative audience. In no time the editors were besieged with subscription requests from big cities and small towns. Noxema recalls that after receiving the 'zine, "one kid from Waukesha, Wis., actually came out in his own 'zine. This was while he was still in high school. I could never have done that when I went to high school in a tiny town. I wasn't together enough."

"That was really inspiring," Rex Boy adds. "It spurred us on, realizing that there were these young kids out there getting rid of *Bimbox*. We were helping them to come out and to plug into a network of other unusual people."

"It's sort of nice to know that *Bimbox* might get to them before they discover *The ADVOCATE* and start growing mustaches and thinking of women as fish on legs," smiles

Noxema.

The *Bimbox* team estimates they've sent out about a thousand copies of each of their past four issues—with articles like "I Was a Sex Object for Gus Van Sant" and a Partridge Family discography as well as pop-up prick and labia posters that got the second issue seized by U.S. customs officials. The 'zine costs $4 to fabricate and $2 to mail.

"Have we spent $24,000?" Noxema grins. "That's insane! But, you know, that's one thing that makes Toronto so comfortable. With the national health program, Rex can trust big ladies and AIDS patients and still make a comfortable living. We can afford to put out this 'zine instead of pumping money into boats or playing golf or investing in nuclear weapons like meat doctors do."

Despite the daunting overhead, *Bimbox* isn't slowing down, though there is some question as to how long they can keep giving away their increasingly ambitious productions to a growing list of devotees. *Bimbox* #1 (the video issue, slated to be distributed on VHS cassette), due out shortly, features Jeffrey Kennedy's Super 8 meditation, *Old Boyfriends*, Candy Parker's short, *The Junk Food Killers*, about punk girls assaulting a junk-food shopper; *The Lollipop Brides*, Noxema's recounting of the making of queer

Canadian camp-a-rave Gloria Jones's spinning kiddie-porn epic; DeAundra Peek's cover of *Stardusty*, Lisa Barlowp's vicious performance piece, and Los Angeles–based "trash" Vaginal Creme Davis's 12-step work shop for those addicted to beauty and glamour.

"We're trying to get away from people thinking that they have to fit into groups," Rex Boy reflects, "whether it's groups of clones or Queer Nation clones. *Bimbox* speaks up for individuality. We spotlight people who have unique voices. Being handicapped and a psychologist, I want to see and to hear from those people."

"And we won't rest," Noxema has vowed, "until we see *Bimbox* on every coffee table in America."

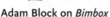

Bimbox coeditor Johnny Noxema (left) and sidekick Rex Boy passing quality toilet time "*Bimbox* is fueled by a lot of anger," says Rex Boy. "But there is a humor that [disbelievers don't get."

2/11/92

Adam Block on *Bimbox*

babies, they hated Vito Russo (understandably), they said after he died of AIDS that he should be dug up and a stake driven through his heart . . . that kind of stuff. They put out an anti-Burroughs fanzine called *Double Bill*. They absolutely hated Williams Burroughs because they believed he murdered his wife and they thought he was a misogynist. They took a really hardcore position. But they also pretty much bought everyone's affections by treating them to expensive dinners and hotel rooms and whatnot, flying people around. Dennis Cooper and G.B. and that whole new cadre were enamored with them, partly for that reason, I presume, but it was pretty ironic. They no longer had to go to Kinko's to publish their zines because the *Bimbox* guys owned their own xerox machine! I think they also had a Bentley or something. They put out some pretty nasty zines, one in particular targeting Candy, for not taking sides in the feud—that was unusually cruel. It deeply wounded her. It sort of started the zine wars and divided the scene. G.B. and I had had this really intense, heavily romantic but platonic relationship for five or six years, but then it all fell apart.

Mykel Board: G.B. Jones and Johnny Noxzema, in a classic punk way, accused Bruce of *selling out*. It's a punk pastime to accuse each other of selling out—it's been a punk pastime since the early '80s. They got pissed off at him for selling out, then he got pissed off at them for calling him a sellout, and it just went on from there. I like both sides—I like Johnny Noxzema, I like Tom Girl of Finland, and I like Bruce, so it's tough.

Dennis Cooper: G.B. came over to Johnny's side and that really infuriated Bruce. And Johnny just completely pushed it, he did actively try to steal Candy and all those people away from Bruce; Johnny was just incredibly talented. And Bruce was brilliant as well. But I got stuck in it because I really, really liked Johnny and you couldn't like both of them. So I did this book called *Discontents*, which was queer punk writing from the zines, and basically Johnny was like, *I will not be in this if Bruce is in it*. And I ultimately made a big mistake by agreeing and not having Bruce in it, which caused all these problems. I admired Johnny tremendously, and I did Bruce as well. But I got on really well with Johnny personally. And Bruce and I . . . I liked Bruce but we never became close friends. We used to correspond. I mean, the first queer punk thing I ever saw was when Bruce sent me a copy of *J.D.s*, and we started corresponding really early on. But personally and aesthetically and temperamentally, I got along really well with Johnny and Rexboy.

Glenn Belverio: That was the G.B. Jones camp, and there was the Bruce LaBruce camp. It was a civil war—we would attack each other through our zines. When I found out that G.B. was going to be in New York I was kind of like, *Oh my god, this is going to be a turf war! She's going to beat me up!* She was at the

Adam Block on G.B. Jones

Pyramid Club, and I think I just went up to her and introduced myself. Of course she knew who I was. She was really charming, really sexy, and it turned out that the *Bimbox* people really respected what we were doing at Pussy Grazer. There was a common ground, because both camps were critiquing the gay mainstream. We were such a small movement, it seemed ridiculous to continue a civil war. So . . . I love what G.B. did with the Tom of Finland drawings. She's great in *No Skin off My Ass*.

Jürgen Brüning: G.B. Jones, who was the codirector of the film, got pissed because Bruce got all the attention for *No Skin off My Ass*. And I thought, *Why is this necessary?* I could understand being pissed, but I said, *Can't we talk about it?* It was impossible. She was so angry with him that they stopped working with each other. And they had worked together for a long time.

But the same kind of thing happened when I did *Hustler White* with Bruce and Rick Castro. I came to Los Angeles for the preproduction, and Rick Castro—the first meeting I had with Bruce and Rick Castro, Rick brought his lawyer. And the first thing he wanted to talk about was, *who's first in the credits? Is it Rick or is it Bruce?* And I thought, *In what world are they living? We are doing a very cheap $50,000 film. It's not even shot.* But in Los Angeles, people want to talk about who's first in the credits.

Bruce LaBruce: There are always issues of credit, and one person getting more attention than another. When I made my first feature film, *No Skin off My Ass*—which was made for absolutely no budget—I shot it for $2,000 and then blew it up to 16mm, so the total budget was like $14,000 or something—and even at that time people thought I was selling out because I was making a $16,000 movie.

It also happened to correspond with the development of the gay and lesbian film festival circuit, so that film really got an international distribution that I was never expecting. G.B. Jones was a main character in the film, and she really kind of just played herself. It was kind of a documentation of our lives. But I never expected it to show outside of Toronto. It was designed to be shown at alternative art spaces and punk clubs, totally underground. And then because of this platform of the gay and lesbian festival circuit, which was just exploding at that time, I got lumped in with the new queer cinema. I got a lot of attention and I was being flown all over the world, and . . . and there was some resentment about that, that I didn't give G.B. Jones enough credit, that I should have given her a writing credit, which I probably should have. That was part of the rift. But it was more of an emotional breakup. Like a divorce, y'know? Everyone gets divorced sooner or later.

We had a very strong, creative, collaborative relationship and, y'know, these things happen when you have that kind of strong emotional bond. We created this whole scene, it became internationally recognized, and then we had a falling out. So it divided people. People took sides with one or the other. Candy, who had this great fanzine *Dr. Smith*, was kind of caught in the middle. And then it became very acrimonious. They started putting out fanzines that were extremely mean-spirited, personal attacks. So that kind of divided the scene down the middle.

Johnny Noxzema: I never understood—I was never really friends with Bruce, ever. My friend Gary was—I think Gary met him in a park, or at a Liza Minnelli concert or something. But I never got to know Bruce that well. During that time I sided with G.B. and I still do, over whatever issues they had over *No Skin off My Ass* or whatever else. Bruce was good in *The Yo Yo Gang*; I haven't seen any of the movies he's done on his own. That's not true—I saw one in the late '90s, there were skinheads in it. But I guess he's doing well for himself, with the whole gay vampire-werewolf-zombie thing that's so popular with teenage girls right now.

Bruce Labruce: Traveling the world, going to fancy film festivals—it's so *glaahmorous*. I mean, what? I'm not living in Bel Air, y'know. I live a very simple life myself. I mean, I'm an artist, I'm a filmmaker, I show my work, I get invited to places to show my work. It's about the content of the work, not the "glamour" of traveling, which can be very actually difficult. You have to go around the world and defend your work, you have to be very social, you have a lot of social obligations. But sometimes you don't even want to be . . . I mean, it's not always what it appears to be.

Scott Treleaven: Historically speaking, whenever you bring people together who are incredibly intelligent and phenomenally creative, splits always happen. Because everyone has to pursue whatever their creative drive is. And it's very rare that a group of people can sustain the same trajectory. It's actually really normal that that happened.

G.B. Jones: It was the same thing when all the Situationists fought, or when Romaine Brooks was fighting with Jean Cocteau, like any creative community full of artists and writers and musicians who don't come from perfect nuclear families in the suburbs. You're talking about a group of people who basically ran away from their dysfunctional homes and were trying to make lives for themselves.

Scott Treleaven: When I made my queercore documentary, people would ask, *So, are you talking about this split?* And my first thought was—again, historically speaking, it's natural and normal and just the way things go. Not particularly interesting to me. And the second thing was, if I was going to be making about a documentary about the *ideology* around queercore, and if I really wanted to perpetuate and *activate* queercore as a concept and make people participate in it, then to set it up in such a way that people felt like there were these *stars*, with some kind of monopoly on the ideas, or that there was this magical group of people and now that they've disbanded everything we're getting is just the dregs, is not useful. It's not helpful, and it would just fix queercore in the past and make it useless to everyone.

Bruce LaBruce: I'm a little more philosophical about these relationships that blow out—supernovas, collaborations that end in a big bang and heavy falling-out. They're kind of a beautiful thing—two like-minded people come together, they kind of fall in love, they're inspired by each other and it spurs them both on to this great creativity. Then there's an inevitable clash, and falling-out—sometimes that happens sooner, sometimes it happens later—and they both go off, like two separate galaxies, in different directions. It's *good*; it's a good thing. You *grow*. I mean, if you stay in the same orbit your whole life you're never going to grow or discover new things. So you have to be kind of philosophical about it. I mean, how many people . . . it's like going through a number of relationships. It's like getting married eight times, like Liz Taylor.

Certain people got very malicious and I don't think I ever got malicious. I think *Super 8½* was an homage to my relationship with G.B. Jones. I think it was very affectionate. There were a few digs, but in general I think it was a kind of melancholy film about a breakup of a creative relationship, a kind of platonic love relationship.

16

CONTAGIOUS EUPHORIA
QUEERCORE ON SCREEN

Glenn Belverio: The *Brenda and Glennda* show started in 1990. The first episode was—it was kind of my segue. I'd been in ACT UP and a lot of queer activist groups, and I wanted to do something that was more fun and creative, that expressed gay politics without being so strident and serious about everything. I wanted to do something that was entertaining. I felt it was the best way to get the message out. So the first show was called *The Out and Outrageous Bus Ride*. It was just a bunch of drag queens; we got on the Ninth Street

Bruce La Bruce on 9 Broadcast Plaza.

Brenda Sexual, Bruce La Bruce and Glennda Orgasm at The New Festival.

A page right out of *Pussy Grazer*

bus, it was really lo-fi, the sound was bad, there was shaky camerawork like the early days of public-access TV. We interviewed people on the bus, we interviewed each other, we told stories, we had this beat poet who read a poem about being out and outrageous. So that was the first show: the whole idea of taking drag out into public, being on the street and forcing people to interact with it instead of lip-synching on a stage in a gay nightclub.

Then we were invited to Hallwalls in Buffalo to do a series of videos for their *Ways in Being Gay* series. We went out with this petition and tried to get people to sign this petition to rename Buffalo *the Queen City*—which is actually true, it used to be nicknamed the Queen City. We got a lot of mixed reactions—people that loved it and people that were kind of offended because they thought "queen" was a derogatory term for gays and they didn't understand what we were doing. And then we went to the mayor's office and tried to present him this petition, and they kicked us out and almost had us arrested. So we were very earnest in the beginning.

Through my show, in 1990, Brenda and I were asked to do an episode of our show at the opening premiere of the film *My Father Is Coming* by Monika Treut. Bruce was also showing *No Skin off My Ass*, and of course we interviewed Bruce because I was huge fan of that film and he was a fan of my drag persona. He didn't really like most drag queens, but what I was doing with Brenda was much different because it was political. And there was the punk background . . . so Bruce and I became friends after I interviewed him on the show. We are both Capricorns, so we really clicked. We have the same personalities and sensibilities, I think.

Bruce LaBruce and I did episodes of the show that really satirized gay culture—like, we went back into the closet, and we wouldn't use the word *queer* anymore because we just felt it was square. We wanted to go back to pre-Stonewall days of gay identity when people were still in the closet, because we felt that gay identity was more interesting then. And [we thought] that homosexuality should be an invisible influence on culture, on films and books, and so on—I still believe that. I felt it was more interesting when it *was* an invisible influence. Now it's like gay people *have* to be stars. Every gay man thinks they're a celebrity. And social media has made it a million times worse. The whole gay marriage thing—like, every little opportunity to put an equal sign. It's really gone back to that early '90s moment where you're not allowed to disagree what the mainstream is thinking on gay politics and gay identity. I just can't be bothered with it anymore.

Bruce and I made a trilogy, which was all about debunking queer identity and moving out to a new identity. There was *The Post Queer Tour*, and then there was *Mondo Toronto*, where I went to Toronto to visit Bruce and he played Liza Minnelli. *A Case for the Closet* was the third part of the trilogy—it also appears in Mark Simpson's book *Anti-Gay*, which is a compilation of gay writers critiquing gay culture. It was this satire where Bruce and I wanted to cure ourselves of our homosexuality because we were just tired of being gay. There's this art cult in New York on Greene St. called the Aesthetic Realists and they do a gay cure.

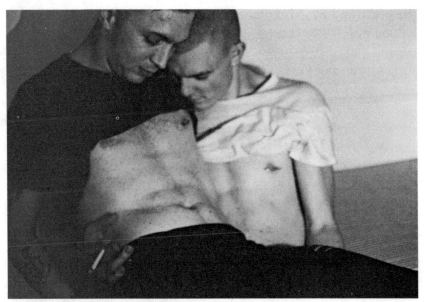

Bruce LaBruce and Klaus von Brucker

We went there in drag, walked into one of their meetings and said that we wanted to be cured. They threw us out . . . After we did that video, I can't remember how many more I did—not many.

Bruce LaBruce: One of the reasons we adopted pseudonyms and had private mailboxes was to elude the authorities, because we were constantly getting harassed by the authorities. For me it started with this one infamous trip that we took to Hallwalls Gallery in Buffalo to show our Super 8 experimental movies, which had pornographic content. We got stopped at the border, and they confiscated our films and watched them—they had Super 8 projectors at the border, they had a "porno room" where these retired cops would sit and watch porn all day. I would get stopped at the border routinely, because I had a mohawk and multiple piercings. They'd take me aside and ask me why I was wearing gloves. They thought I was covering up my jailhouse tattoos or something.

And then film labs starting calling. I had a lab for *No Skin off My Ass* when I had the film blown up to 16mm, and the lab owner called the cops, and the cops came and looked at the film and wanted to destroy the negatives. They objected to scenes with S&M—I think S&M, bondage with violence, and sucking of toes were the three offending sections. But I managed to get to get it back from the lab owner without destroying the negative. I had also photographic labs call the cops. This was all around 1990.

Jürgen Brüning: I met Bruce in '89 when I was working Hallwall's, where I was programming films and inviting a lot of younger experimental filmmakers from Toronto. And people were saying, *There's this interesting young Super 8 filmmaker in Toronto named Bruce LaBruce, and you should meet him.* So eventually I went to Toronto to party, because Buffalo is a really a dead city after about six o'clock. And at one party in Toronto I got introduced to Bruce. We said hi to each other and then both turned away. We were a little bit snobbish to each other.

Some months later I was in San Francisco shooting a film called *What Is the Relationship Between Rosa Von Praunheim and the Male Strippers in San Francisco?* Bruce was in town while I was shooting, and I invited him to the set. It was much more relaxed, and we talked, and he told me he had a project that he wanted to shoot. He sent me, like, two or three pages—this was the script for *No Skin off My Ass.* I said, *OK, let's do it,* and I gave him a little money. They were shooting on Super 8 and it took more than a year before I saw something. When I did see something I thought, *This looks interesting*—but with Super 8 you can only do so much. So a friend of mine in Berlin blew the film up to 16mm, and then a friend of Bruce's

A poster for *No Skin off My Ass* from Japan

who was programming a film festival in London of experimental sci-fi showed the film and it became this underground tape. Amy Taubin from the *Village Voice* wrote about it and compared it to Andy Warhol's early work and blah blah blah, and suddenly people were talking about it and it got shown everywhere.

Critics always need references. But . . . I mean, there was a group of people working together, like in Andy Warhol's films, and Bruce was, y'know, the *head*—but you always have that in film. Fassbinder had his main group of people that he was working with in the late '60s, who he was exploiting. Andy Warhol did the same, and Bruce LaBruce did the same. But they were documenting their time and their surroundings. Your inspiration is where you live and what you are, and this goes into your film. Bruce is aware of art history—so he knew, for sure, what Andy Warhol did and that he didn't want to be a copy of Warhol. He wanted to make his own stuff. But he was aware of how Warhol presented himself, merchandised himself, and so on.

I don't think Bruce is using pornography in his films. When you have an explicit sex scene, people will say that it's pornography. But experimental film has *always* had explicit scenes. Jean Genet, Kenneth Anger, Jack Smith, even Andy Warhol. Or Barbara Hammer. These films are not pornographic films. But sexuality is still so taboo. Our capitalist society fears free sexuality, therefore it's labeled pornography, and it's considered sleazy and degrading. And most pornography, which is commercially produced, *is* degrading, *is* exploitative. But this is changing, too. Because there are more and more people making their own pornography, making their own sexual films—queer filmmaker Courtney Trouble in San Francisco; Petra Joy, who's catering to a different sort of audience in London; Emilie Jouvet in Paris; Marit Östberg in Berlin.

Bruce LaBruce: My position on pornography is that, in some ways, I think that gay pornographers are the last radicals, the last gay radicals. The gay movement used to be thoroughly radicalized by intense sexual expression, it was kind of the motor that drove the gay movement. And that doesn't seem to be the case so much anymore. The gay conservative movement has distanced itself from a lot of the extreme sexuality in the scene, so in some ways, I see gay porn stars as the last radicals. And I express solidarity with pornographers. I think a lot of people look down their noses at pornographers and don't really appreciate what they do.

When I make porn films—y'know, you quickly realize that shooting the porn, the actual sex scenes, is the least interesting part of the whole process. I'm more interested in making the style of porn where there's a lot of other things going on—the narrative, the characters, trying to concentrate on aesthetics. So yeah, I quite often just let my producer shoot the sex scenes. For anyone who's ever been on a porn shoot, it's not a very sexual environment, really. It's kind of an awkward environment.

It's kind of boring to shoot sex. It's very hard to shoot sex and make it look interesting. There's only so much you can do. So . . . that's usually when I take my lunch break.

Bruce Benderson: I think that Bruce is—in a good way—a reluctant pornographer, who enjoys certain charlatan-like activities. He likes to trick people. I don't see Bruce as a deeply committed political person; I don't see Bruce going to Iran to sneak out gays who've been condemned to death. I see Bruce as an artist and pleasure seeker, and a trickster—and a very interesting one.

Kembra Pfahler: The tone of Bruce's films can be hysterical and can drive you almost to a point of mania, or what Vaginal Davis calls *drag fever*. You just get so overstimulated to the point that you get drag fever. It's a kind of contagious euphoria that you get from watching. The way he presented sexuality was something that I could identify with so much more than anything else I've seen on film. Even though it was mostly dudes being with each other, I felt like, *Wow, Bruce is really capturing something that I find so sexy.*

I remember when I was making S&M films in the '90s, I used to work at this place called Gotham Gold Studios in Queens, and that was one of the ways—it was, like, my day job, and we would have to make like six sexy adult feature films in order for me to make one of my own Karen Black films. So I'd go in and I'd have different scenarios, and I'd provide the film company with all these (what I perceived to be) sexy feature films. We got into so much trouble because I just hired my friends, and we didn't change our appearances, we didn't look like Barbie dolls. I remember so often the film producers would shut the set down. They kept saying, *Is this sexy? Are you sure this is sexy?* I'm like, *Yeah, yeah, it's great. It's sexy.* It was very unhinged what we did in those S&M films. I think it's just up to the individual, what people think is sexy or not, y'know.

Jürgen Brüning: In the beginning, of course, Bruce's films were shown at lesbian and gay festivals. Then the big international festivals—like, *Hustler White* was shown at the Berlin Film Festival and at Sundance Festival. Then Bruce's films started being shown in Australia, and Japan, and also in countries that are in certain ways more oppressive—like,

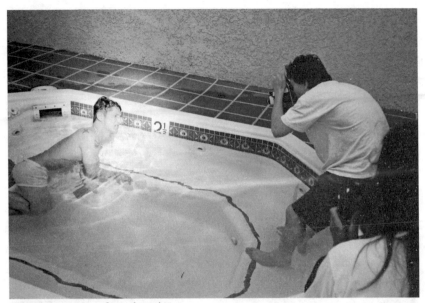

Behind the scenes of *Hustler White*

some years ago a festival in Istanbul asked me if they could show *Raspberry Reich*. I said, *Are you sure?* Because, y'know, it's explicit. It has homosexuality in it. It has explicit straight sex and explicit gay sex in it. They said yes. So I had to change my prejudice in thinking of Turkey as a Muslim country where things would be very difficult.

But still, commercially, Bruce's films are very difficult to sell because of certain legal things—his films being labeled as pornography, so they can only be sold as porn films. In some countries you can sell porn only in certain shops, like in Germany. In other countries like England there are specific laws saying you can only show consensual sex. Like, when you have the rape scene, there's no consent in that so you have to cut it out. So his films are getting . . . how do you say this in English, mutilated? Cut. At a certain point while I was working with Bruce, y'know, distribution companies would asked us, *Can we cut into the film? Because we can't show this scene in our country.* I had a long talk with Bruce, and we agreed—OK, in festivals we'll show only the original versions. Because this is what we want to show, what people should see. But when it goes into the commercial world, like distribution companies, we agree that the person in England can cut this scene, the person in Australia can cut that scene. And it's still going on. The big thing in Australia was *L.A. Zombie*. Every film in Australia has to be viewed by the classification

G.B. Jones among the stars (in her room)

board. The classification board in Australia declared that the film was not suitable for any audience in Australia, so it was banned totally in Australia. And it had an invitation for the Melbourne International Film Festival! So they pulled the film out, and it became a scandal, of course. There was this guy from the Melbourne Underground Film Festival who wanted to show it, and he showed it illegally and got a court case. So, y'know, it's like this with every film. In the '80s I worked with Richard Kern and Lydia Lunch, and we presented *Fingered* in Berlin. Where there's also a rape scene, Lydia is raping a woman with a gun. And this caused a big controversy in Germany. So my production career, my film career, is filled with these episodes where people are always opposing the films I produce.

G.B. Jones: When I was living in my apartment on Parliament Street, which you can see in *The Troublemakers,* and there was a hole in the ceiling and the raccoons were falling through, it was not necessarily easy to convince people to come to my house to make a movie. Because at first sight, the impression was not of someone who was going to be very successful or helpful in establishing a career for upcoming actors, or writers or musicians. In fact it was quite the opposite. So I have to give a lot of credit to people who were actually brave enough, and exciting enough, to work with us in the first place.

Mark Freitas: G.B. Jones is interesting as a director. I'm in her movie *The Yo-Yo Gang*, and I do a sort of PG-13, almost-X-rated sex scene with Bruce LaBruce's then-boyfriend Klaus von Brucker. She was working with an 8 mm camera, and she only had a tiny bit of film, five or ten minutes of film, so she had this very exact choreography—this super-frantic thing where we're doing every position known to man, very quickly. We practiced for two hours to get it down. Everybody's like, *Did she undercrank the camera?* It looks sped-up, but we were actually moving that fast. She knew exactly what she wanted, though, she had everything choreographed. It took her, what, three, four years to make that movie?

A poster for *The Troublemakers*

Larry-Bob Roberts: G.B. works slowly on film projects. It took years and years for G.B.'s movies *The Yo-Yo Gang* and *The Lollipop Generation* to come out. They're Super 8 movies, y'know, really true to the aesthetic of do-it-yourself. You'll see people in these movies and it's like, *Wow, I remember when this person used to have hair, and they're bald now.* This is how long these movies take.

Kathleen Hanna: There was always a sense of humor in all of G.B. Jones's movies. We were completely influenced by that stuff, *Yo-Yo Gang* and *the Troublemakers*—we were always trying to find Anti-Scrunti Faction, which was Leslie Mah from Tribe 8's band, because we saw them in the movie, then we got a tape of them and were like, *Where are these girls, we have to be friends with them!*

17

SMOKE SIGNALS
THEATER AND PERFORMANCE

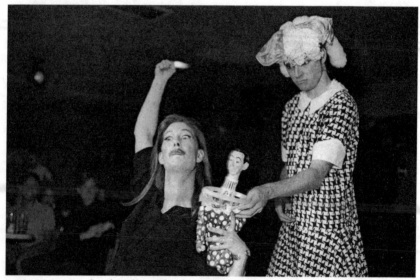

Justin Vivian Bond and Rodney O'Neil Austin at Klubstitute, 1991. Photo by Daniel Nicoletta

Justin Vivian Bond: I remember reading Greil Marcus's *Lipstick Traces*, which was about the Situationist movement, and he gave this historical context which went back to the Cabaret Voltaire, and *cabaret*—cabaret started out as punk, Brecht and all that. I mean, Brecht's original one-act play of *The Rise and Fall of the City of Mahagonny* was about the prostitutes going in and taking over the city—the sex workers rebelling, a revolution of sexuality, which was what was happening during the Weimar era, before Hitler, this outrageous rising-up of queer communities and sex workers. I think punk wasn't something that originated in London in the late '70s, it was something that went back further than that, and it was also kind of queer in that regard. So I had been always been attracted to the punk attitude if not necessarily to the aesthetic.

I moved to San Francisco in 1988, and I was going to establish residence in California and become an art history major. Then I found out about Theater Rhinoceros, which is the oldest continuous queer theater company in the US, and I auditioned for a show. And while I was doing this play, Kate Bornstein came backstage and gave me her script for *Hidden: A Gender*, which was this groundbreaking play about gender and her personal history of being a "heterosexual" man becoming a transsexual lesbian. I played Herculine Barbin, a nineteenth-century French hermaphrodite, and that was when I really started to getting into my own exploration of gender, which I'd been trying to shove under the rug.

The only thing I knew was I "had" to be a man or a woman. There wasn't the language for what I was. And then we went to Seattle for the national gay and lesbian theater festival there, it might have been the first. And it just so happened that Holly Hughes, Karen Finley, John Fleck, Tim Miller, Split Britches, Peggy Shaw, Lois Weaver—all these legendary queer artists were there. So I was suddenly initiated into the politics of queer culture, queer performance, and queer arts. And I decided that was what I was: I was a queer artist. So from that point on, everything I've done has been through the lens of being a queer performance artist, but also an activist. Because I realized how political being queer was, and being transgender was, and how threatening it was. Literally, at that time, it seemed that the US government wanted all queer people dead. And they were defunding our art and saying that we were going to burn in hell. People were showing up at our performances—protestors, right-wing fanatical Christians, harassing us and trying to silence us, which just meant it was even more important for us to be loud.

Kembra Pfahler: Performance, for me, is a way of sending smoke signals. It wasn't about entertainment at all, when I started; it was about availablism, making the best use of what's available. It originated from not having any money. *What are you going to use? What's available?* I have my body and my ideas. So I began with this really minimal sort of body-oriented performance work.

The first thing that I did—I remember I was just walking down the street one day and someone asked if I would do a performance art piece

Vaginal Davis kisses the crowd

at a club or something. I said yes and I went home and tried to decide what I would do, because I had no idea what I would do. I always hated showbusiness; I never wanted to be in theater at all. In fact, I couldn't stand theater, I would feel so uncomfortable watching plays or certain kinds of movies that I would just cringe. So I didn't come to performance as a way of entertaining people; my early performance work wasn't entertaining at all. Performance was just a low-tech, do-it-yourself way of presenting an idea to a group of people. And I didn't know a lot about performance when I started doing it; I didn't know about Yoko Ono's cutting piece where she cut off her clothes, I didn't know about Joseph Beuys's piece where he sat in a room with a wolf. The only performance stuff that I'd seen were the punk bands—there were what would be considered performance-art elements to that work.

So performance was about availabism, for me. And it was also really fun to do. It's definitely a way to overcome shyness. I was always extremely shy, and I cured myself of that; I cured myself of body shame by being naked so often. I heartily recommend it to people instead of therapy.

Performance is immaterial, it can't really be monetized. So it's always a problem for people in the art world, for collectors; an audience sometimes just doesn't know what to do with such a strong, impactful presentation. I think people don't know how to process it. A lot of great art is dismissed as just being done for shock value. It's just a way of not looking at something, hiding it from it or being afraid to process it. It's funny, I don't think of what I do as being shocking at all. Sort of dark vanilla.

Mark Freitas: I think performance has always been a part of punk. Iggy Pop was playing with gender in the '60s, playing with performance art . . . Jayne County is very much a performance artist . . .

Martín Sorrondeguy: I mean, the Dicks were definitely doing "performance." Gary Floyd was phenomenal at putting himself out there in ways that made the *punks* uncomfortable! And I think that's what appealed to so many of us—those few performers who really *pushed*. They called themselves a *commie faggot band*—in *Texas*, in 1979. They started as a flyer band, where they were just making flyers—like, *The Dicks Are Coming!*, y'know, and they would put them up all over town. But they ended up forming a real band, and they were phenomenal. Gary was very large, he would wear dresses, makeup, he didn't give a shit. They were good friends with the Big Boys, and they were all super queer. And it took punk, that era of punk, by surprise—this was *Texas*. Texas is super-conservative—and here's all these young people, fucking with *everything*.

Bands like that would go touring, go to California or whatever, and make *punks* feel weird—and I think that was the beauty of queer punk, that it really made punk *punk* again. I think I pull from that when I perform. If the scene or the crowd gets too tough, I feel like I *have* to fuck with them. I have to make the toughest guy feel a little weird.

18

MANUFACTURING GAY
ASSIMILATION AND ITS DISCONTENTS

San Francisco Gay Pride, No Assimilation Contingent, June 24, 1990

Justin Vivian Bond: When I was in San Francisco in the early '90s they'd already started manufacturing *gay*. I remember when those freedom rings came into the bookstore where I worked; and the queens at A Different Light were *not* having those freedom rings—freedom rings with dog tags and all of this stuff, and we just wanted to throw up, it was so disgusting.

Sarah Schulman: I think it's a part of AIDS trauma. AIDS made gay people visible, because people *visibly* had AIDS and visibly died. Prior to AIDS, the culture pretended that queer people didn't exist. Suddenly they could never again claim that we didn't exist. Suddenly everybody knew somebody who was gay; suddenly everyone knew they had someone gay in their family. So their whole sense of their supremacy had to shift; they had to reinvent their supremacy. And they reinvented it as this idea that *the more you resemble us the more we'll accept you—on our terms.* And that's a consequence of the AIDS crisis. If there had not been an AIDS crisis, the sexual revolution would have continued.

The goal of gay liberation was to expand what is possible for a human being, to open up the society and make all different ways of living, and all different ways of being sexual and being in a relationship and being in a community, accessible and possible for all people. Eventually this movement, as the country and the world became more reactionary, was replaced by a gay *rights* movement. And that's an entirely different idea. It's not about social transformation; it's about gay people fitting into already-existing social concepts of what is acceptable. So what we have now is that instead of gay people, or queer people, changing the world, the world has changed *us.* Now we become acceptable to the degree that we resemble the dominant culture.

When Barack Obama says that we should respect gay people because we should respect *love,* what he's talking about is gay marriage and gay family structure, which is what love means to him. He is not talking about sexual liberation at all, and he's not talking about even the basics of antidiscrimination laws. He's talking about us fitting *exactly* into his concept of how a citizen should behave. Herbert Marcuse called that *repressive tolerance*—when you're *tolerated,* which keeps you in a position of subservience and inferiority at the will and whim of the dominant group. And this is being touted, hours after Obama's speech, as this revolutionary concept that shows that gay people have *arrived.* But actually it shows that we're in terrible trouble. Because on our own, in the places where we are different from dominant culture, there's no acceptance at all.

Bruce LaBruce: It's kind of ironic that back in the 1980s we used to think that the gay clones from the '70s were so horrible and pathetic. They were, y'know, these creatures who would all dress the same, the same gay uniform with the white T-shirt and high-waisted jeans and all that—the clone look. Now that seems so glamorous, somehow—that there was this kind of militant uniform, and that sex was the engine of the gay movement, it was all about sexual revolution and sexual radicalism. That probably doesn't make sense anymore; y'know, AIDS wrecked *that* party, so . . . but now there's a new kind of sexual conformity. I think that there are still some people who are oppositional and doing interesting, insane things. But it's not, like, a cohesive, militant movement; it's individuals here and there.

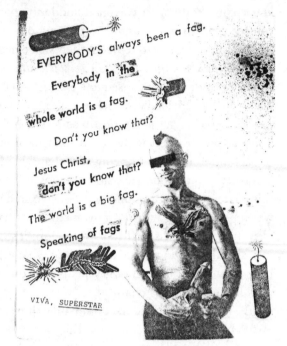

EVERYBODY'S always been a fag. Everybody in the whole world is a fag. Don't you know that? Jesus Christ, don't you know that? The world is a big fag. Speaking of fags

VIVA, SUPERSTAR

You know what you are . . . from *J.D.s* no. 2

Mads Ananda Lodahl: One of the big differences between assimilationist strategies and queer strategies is in shifting your focus away from *yourself*, and away from the people who deviate, all the queers and the freaks, and turning it toward the structure, the system, and the people who represent it. For example, you stop *defending homosexuality* and you start *attacking homophobia*. There's a big difference.

Lynn Breedlove: Tom Jennings had a giant banner up in his house at 666 Illinois in San Francisco that said *No Assimilation Ever*. Now . . . TV shows like *Will & Grace* and *Glee* are all about, *Look how cute we are. We're gay—don't you love us? We're so cute. If God hates fags, why are we so cute?* Which is one way—and it's a very important way—to bring visibility and awareness about queers, to be like, *Look, we're charming. We're cute. We're just like you. Look how adorable we are and how sexy.*

But *we* were like, *Yeah, we're queer; you hate us, right? Yeah, we're that. We're that thing you hate.* And people . . . I guess it's the same reason you pay money to go on a rollercoaster, because it's scary—we pay to be scared. And people wanted that. Sometimes you want *Will & Grace*, sometimes you want Tribe 8. Like we always say, there's room for Melissa

Etheridge and there's room for Tribe 8, but you need both. You come at the problem from all directions, y'know; from the mellifluous sounds of Melissa Etheridge, singing about climbing through some babe's window, to us being like, *Suck my dick, motherfucker!* You need both.

Scott Treleaven: One of the great attracting forces of queercore, at the time, was that it was basically indigestible. The last thing people wanted was a bunch of fags that only knew three chords—or less—banging on their guitars and singing about how great it is to fuck dudes or chicks chasing each other around with dildos, cutting them off with chainsaws and things like that—capitalism was not really prepared for that. Now? I don't know; probably yes. Being the creature that it is, it eventually digests everything.

At the time though, it was only, like, small record stores and really indie places where you could find this stuff. Not only that, but there was a whole economy that didn't even interface with things like record labels. You had zines all over the place, and they were just made by someone out of their bedroom. So it was definitely an alternative economy. Swapping was a big thing. *You have a band? Great, me too—I'll swap your cassette for mine.* Money went out of the window in a lot places.

Silas Howard: Once the mainstream media got ahold of it, they fucked it up, y'know. It was like the Year of Queercore, and the sentiment was, *Well, this is cool, but how long can you sing about drugs and sex and misguided love?*—as though rock 'n' roll wasn't *always* about drugs and love and all that. Rolling Stone did an article about queercore—Tribe 8 and Pansy Division, some other bands, and the tone was like—I remember there was a picture of us, with our '90s tattoos and leather pants and tank tops, and underneath it said, like, *lesbian, knife-wielding, men-hating* . . . it was like an *Attack of the 50-Foot Woman* kind of sentiment. And it just talked shit about how the bands hated each other, and then ended by asking, like, how long can queers sing about themselves and hold our interest?

Lynn Breedlove: *Rolling Stone* magazine put us in there as, like, the next big thing one year. We were really excited and we had long conversations in the van about whether or not we were going to accept any offers to get signed to a major label and all that. I was always like, *No, don't be a sellout. We're punk rock!* And Silas was like, *Why not? Let's make some* *money!* But . . . they weren't exactly beating our doors down. So we didn't have to go there.

G.B. Jones: At a certain point, MTV and some of the larger institutions started to get interested because it seemed like it was going to become a really big trend. But it didn't, because middle America was not ready for it, and probably never will be. Kids—queer kids—that's scary for them. It's fine to imagine two gay people getting married and living in the suburbs with a picket fence and getting a nice job as an interior decorator; but queer kids running around, playing punk rock—no, it wasn't going to happen.

Penny Arcade: Every single thing that I've ever been involved with has become commodified—and has left me behind. And that's what happens. But, I mean, pretty soon it won't matter, because there's not going to be any money. The *beautiful, nonviolent, anarchist revolution*—that's Judith Malina, from the Living Theatre. She's eighty-five years old. I was talking with her the other day, and I said, *Now we just have to add the word* queer. The beautiful, non-violent, anarchist, *queer* revolution is coming any moment. Because what's going on in the world financially can't keep going, it can't sustain itself. Then it's going to be *really* DIY, then it's *really* going to be the end of commodity.

Justin Vivian Bond: I always talk about the luxury of normality. The first time *I* experienced the luxury of normality was in the late '90s, when I went to a Radical Faerie gathering. I was not well known to the Radical Faeries—I hadn't starred on Broadway, hadn't been nominated for a Tony, hadn't played Carnegie Hall, this was before all of that. So I went to a Faerie sanctuary, it was my first night there, and I put on this gold lamé dress to go to dinner. And as I was walking through the camp, there were all these people dressed in amazing, outlandish, gorgeous ways, and nobody batted an eye when I walked past. I was used to being stared at, my whole life—either the object of misogynistic comments or homophobic comments, sometimes twice in ten minutes, by different people who perceived me in different ways. No one batted an eye, and I was so shocked, because I had never been invisible before. I burst into tears—it was such a profound thing, to understand what it's like for most people to just walk down the street and not cause a stir.

So I understand the desire to assimilate. I understand the desire to be a man who lives with your husband and your children in a suburban neighborhood. It's a comfortable, safe lifestyle, and I wouldn't begrudge anyone a comfortable, safe lifestyle. I mean, I would like to have a comfortable, safe lifestyle myself; and maybe someday I *will* be more invisible. I think as I get older and I read more as a sort of well-off, middle-aged white woman, I *am* more invisible, which I like. But that doesn't change people's reactions to finding out my truth, and for me, my truth is the most important thing.

And that has nothing to do with assimilation or queer politics; it's a demand that I put on *myself* to be honest, and to grow, and to be able to change, and to not be stuck in an idea that someone else has of me—whether it's my parents, or a current lover, or what I think a future lover might want from me, or my public, as an artist. So I think the idea of being assimilationist is vilified unfairly. But I also don't think that demanding a space to be yourself should be considered a threat to anybody. I call it, like, *expanding the circle of normality*.

Scott Treleaven: I think assimilation helps certain people, and the pain and suffering that certain people go through is alleviated to some degree by assimilation. So I can't be 100 percent anti-assimilationist, because I know that some people, their biggest desire is to simply interact with their fellow human beings in the most fundamental and normal way possible. And for certain people I think that's a source of great stability, and great self-assurance. For other people though, it actually obstructs what might otherwise be a push for a more humane culture, a more open culture, a more accepting culture—even a more mature or wiser culture. All assimilation does is head things off at the pass; it prevents any growth or any further movement or evolution. I mean, if you think that we've achieved everything society can achieve, with our family, church, political structures, police, jail, and so on—if you think that's perfection, then assimilation is the way to go. You should absolutely join them. If you think something is better or could be better—that we can evolve as species—then it's your obligation to resist.

Sara Marcus: I think what was so important about queercore, in the '90s—this was a time when gay rights were within reach, the first real wave of gay rights laws were being passed, and there was a sense that

Homocore Chicago . . . Stonewall Was a Riot Not a Brand Name. Photo by Mark Freitas

things might be moving forward. And then immediately there was a sense that the price of that was going to be *being normal*. Bruce Bawer's book *A Place at the Table*, Andrew Sullivan's *Virtually Normal*—that was all mid-1990s, and it was all this idea, like, *If we can just put the specter of Queer Nation behind us, put the specter of those angry ACT UP people behind us, y'know, stop wearing the crazy chaps at the gay pride parade and be just like regular Americans but gay, then we'll get everything we want.* That was the hegemonic language around having a "liberated" gay life—which *isn't* particularly liberated. And queercore comes in with this completely *other* way. Jody Bleyle's line about *If I wasn't born gay, I'd definitely choose to be* is messing with the whole *We didn't choose this!* approach. Y'know, Team Dresch comes in and says *fuck that*. It creates this whole range of other ways that you can envision your life as liberated person with queer desires.

Deke Nihilson: Some people thought that assimilation, while maybe not for them, was culturally the right way to go—to sort of take the animus out of homophobia, the whole Harvey Milk idea that people who know homosexuals don't hate homosexuals, so the best thing you can do is to come out, because it normalizes homosexuality in the eyes of people who are otherwise scared of it or hate it.

Others of us felt like assimilation into a death culture was itself a death trap. You demand the right to serve in the military and you're going to end up dropping phosphorous bombs on Afghani kids. And really, is that liberation? Is that freedom? Is having a seat at a table of empire really liberation? If you get to run Abu Ghraib and you get to sexually torture and humiliate people, does that mean that you're equal? Because now any American kid can join the army and go make butt pyramids in Iraq. We felt like at its strongest, queer culture represented a standing critique of the entire society and its illnesses and what need to be overthrown—a much more revolutionary take on the potential of queer liberation. And in fact queer liberation represents a sexual liberation for everyone, including straights.

19

A HERD OF CATS
THE QUEERCORE "AGENDA"

Talkin' Shit

I quit working for Maximum Rock'n'Roll magazine after three years of reviews, the occasional column, and the "queer" themed issue. It was a hard decision to make, since working there was not only fun, but also very beneficial and full of perks. I decided it wasn't worth it.

I've always been aware of the reactionary, conservative elements in the mag., but I guess I thought of myself as being somewhat subversive for working within such a structure. It's certainly been vital for promoting stuff like this zine you're reading. However, I too have to draw the line somewhere, and I was forced to do it. After a seemingly endless barrage of SWM's and their paranoid, uptight, and prejudiced columns, comes a new columnist of the same sort. Now that's what I call variety! This guy, "Rev Norb" not only can't write, but has made/continues to make some of the most ignorant, racist/sexist/homophobic statements I have ever read in a "progressive" magazine. And all the "editor" can do is claim he has no control over content and that the readers are free to comment. Well, many have complained, and letters protesting this moronic crap have gone all but unanswered. And to think a columnist was dismissed within the last year for being "too right-wing" - but racism isn't right-wing? Enough of the fence-sitting and the tired, unchallenging old boys' network. Talk about chickenshit! Before all this happened, I was told that the magazine was going to take on a new direction, one that would "shake things up" and challenge people. Why can't we have the guts to "shake things up" on our own turf?

Maybe I've been fooling myself all along. Maybe I was too blind to see it before. Maybe the below record cover best sums it up. Who made these stupid rules, anyway? Fuck this shit.

So retro, it's not funny anymore.

GUN 'EM DOWN!

LOOKING FOR STRAIGHT-ACTING GAYS

Outpunk no. 7

Bruce LaBruce: I like the idea of a homosexual agenda. I think it sounds intimidating. My philosophy of homosexuality has always been to embrace the things that make you different, to embrace the more radical aspects of gay identity. My gay heroes, my cinematic heroes, have always been complete mavericks and crazy people, from Kenneth Anger to Jack Smith, to Warhol and Paul Morrissey, to the Kuchar brothers, to Curt McDowell—and then, y'know, the porn people, like Fred

Halsted, Peter de Rome, and Wakefield Poole. They were avant-gardists; they were underground and weren't interested in orthodox gay politics.

But the idea of a homosexual agenda—it sounds like you're actively trying to recruit straight people into homosexuality. Which I think is a great pastime. I think it's a really worthy goal. So why not? There's always been this perception that gays are this kind of predatory animal—which I think is quite exciting. There used to be an antigay organization on my university campus called the League Against Homosexuals and their motto was, *Queers don't produce, they seduce.* And I always thought, *Wow, that makes us sound really exciting.* So I like the idea of embracing the negative stereotypes that straight society has about homosexuals and really sticking to them.

Cookie: I don't think there was ever, like, an explicit agenda in queer punk, except to say, *You think straight is superior, well we think being queer is superior so fuck you.* Beyond that I'm not really sure what the agenda was. Maybe I just didn't get the memo. I wasn't at that meeting.

Brontez Purnell: Gay is a personal choice. You're going to have to do the hard work like I did. I fucking went through enemy lines, jogged through a mine field, crossed barbed wire, swam through a shark-filled moat to be gay. So if you're not prepared to do that, I'm not going to put you on my back and take you there. I grew up gay in Southern and Baptist Alabama. I mean, gay is something I always was internally, but as a political identity, you either definitely choose it or you definitely don't. I think people have sex with whoever they want, but gay as an identity is not just who you have sex with; it's how you live your life, how you present in the world. Gay is not just who you're having sex with; it's a whole other list of criteria.

Deke Nihilson: By its very nature, queercore is a herd of cats. People who call themselves queer tend to be aggressively individualistic, y'know? *I don't want to be male or female. Why do I have to fit in your paradigm? I want to be who I am, and that might be some of both or neither or something else at any given moment. My gender, my body, my expression is mine to define.* But that's the thing; for all the differences, there is that unifying idea, that unifying unmet need. None of us can be that or do that alone, because it leaves us too isolated, which leaves too many of us vulnerable—which leaves too many of us dead at the hands of haters. So we come together. Not just despite but *because* of our differences, because together we can do things that we can't do alone.

Not all punk rock scenes are like this. My experience has been that big-city punk scenes are actually—like in the Bay Area, there's not *a* scene; there are ten thousand microscenes. There are so many people, so many kinds of punk rock, that you have the luxury of picking and choosing—*Well, who do I want to be friends with? What kind of shows do I want to go to? Who do I want to—or not want to—be around?* I'm from a small, midwestern punk rock scene that was much more like queercore in that it was self-inclusive. If you showed up, you belonged there. If you said you were a part of it, nobody was in the position to say that you weren't. I mean, we had street punks, and suburban kids, and Catholic girl school ejectees, and art students, and mental health outpatients, and burned-out old hippies, and, y'know, the occasional queer. Whoever showed up at a show belonged there. If you made yourself a part of it, you were part of it. You needed everybody you could get around you.

I had a friend, we lived in Midtown, and one night he got shoved headfirst into a trash can, in his own neighborhood. By some drunken suburban cowboy who drove in on his family's flatbed to go get drunk on Coors Light and beat up some faggot punk. My friend didn't have to be a faggot, he just had to *look* different to get treated like one. So we banded together, for survival. And I think that's what a movement like queercore offers. It doesn't offer a uniform. It doesn't offer a common ideology. It's a survival strategy. It created that kind of space where people could come together regardless of whatever else they had going on. And we could survive, and even thrive, through mutual aid and helping each other. Whether we agreed with each other, or even liked each other, or not.

Larry-Bob Roberts: It wasn't a movement that had political goals. Queercore's goals were more about cultural goals than political goals. It was different from assimilationist gay movements, and its goal was not just to be accepted or to be able to accumulate wealth as well or better than straight people. It was more about being able to self-express and to connect with other people.

Justin Vivian Bond: I feel like by being honest and being my authentic self, by performing and sharing what I actually think my world is about, people are being subjected to a queer worldview. And they might not understand it at first, but lots of straight people who come are like, *Oh my god, I feel like I'll never look at the world in the same way again.* It's a worldview that people can only know about if you make them look it. So in that regard, the homosexual agenda for me is just making people see that their way of looking things is not the only way. It's not as provocative as saying, *We're going to turn all your children into homos;* but basically we can make them *think* as homos, even if we can't get them to suck our penises or whatever, our latex penises.

Phranc: Nothing irks me more than seeing—like, my Wikipedia page says *American songwriter.* I was *never* an *American songwriter!* I want to be known as the *Jewish lesbian folk singer.* I want to say the word *Jewish;* I want to say the word *lesbian;* I want to be known as a dyke the minute I walk out the door, every single day. Because I feel like being myself is the most political thing I can do.

20

ALL THE LABELS
NAVIGATING GENDER

Jayne County: I had read, when I was a teenager, every book I could on trans and gay people. One of the biggest had to be John Rechy's *City of Night*. I identified immediately with the drag queens out of that book—Darling Dolly Dane, Miss Destiny. Another big influence for me was the French drag queens of the time, like Coccinelle. She was unbelievable. But I also listened to a lot of old blues music growing up. When I was a teenager everybody else was listening to Frankie Avalon—I was listening to Muddy Waters and Howlin' Wolf. So it's a weird combination. I take the tranny thing—it's like, I'm feminine, standing there in a blonde wig, but then I open up my mouth and I sound like an old blues singer.

I never came out. People go, *When did you come out? Did you come out as gay? Did you come out as tranny?* I was always out. I always just did what I wanted.

I've just been through *all* the labels. When I first came out I came out as gay, then I came out as a transvestite. Then I realized I was more transgender, and then I came out as transsexual. But now I think that *all* the terms are kind of dated. I prefer *gender-variant* now. And I think it's all under the gay banner. The gay, lesbian, bisexual, and transgender community—I think that's a good way of putting it, because the terminology has changed so much. In the '50s and '60s there was no such thing—I mean, everyone was just *gay*. You weren't a drag queen, you weren't a lesbian, you weren't this or that; everyone was *gay*. Later on, everybody wanted their own labels, and it's become very confusing! I can imagine how confusing it is for straight people, because it's confusing for *anyone*, gay or transgender or anything—and the terminology keeps changing. But I would consider myself gender-variant. My gender *varies*, and it varies from time to time. I can't take one label and say, *That's me* and it's always been me; it's always going to be me. With me, it's not like that. And I don't like to be pinpointed either, y'know. The minute people think they've pinpointed me, I change.

I've been told that I opened doors. I have a shy streak. My manager goes, *You shouldn't be like that. You're a pioneer; you were doing stuff before other people were doing it. You should be proud.* And I am proud. But I'm—my manager says, *You're way too humble.* I'm freaky Jayne County but I grew up in the Methodist

Joan Jett Blakk at SPEW at Randolph Street Gallery in Chicago, 1991. Photo by Mark Freitas

church, and I still have a lot of that baggage. I don't like to brag. But I do feel that I am a type of a pioneer, and I hope that what I did helped pave the way and make it easier for other people to travel down that road.

Lynn Breedlove: I remember there was a moment when Slade was like, *What if I transitioned?* And I was like, *Then you can't be in the band, because it's a* dyke *band!* Which was a little bit transphobic, I guess, but it was early on, in the '90s. Yeah, we had friends who were transitioning, but I was stuck in the definition of Tribe 8: *We're a* dyke *band; we are by, for, and about dykes, get it? No dudes allowed!*

And then later, as I watched my friends transition, I was like, *Oh, yeah. That* is *kind of what I want to do.* I never did, like, medically transition, for a number of reasons—money . . . But various choices—a lot of mental stuff and a lot of physical stuff just lined up to where I was like,

Y'know what? I'm a dude. I've always been a dude. People who transition say they've been dudes all along; they're just making the outside match the inside. Well, what if I *don't* make the outside match the inside, and I just challenge you? Like, *Y'know what? I'm not going to make the outside match the inside. I'm just going to tell you who I am.* And that's the way it's always been—my outsides and my insides are *always* at odds.

I think there's an evolutionary process. I mean, I was out there—basically, the idea of taking our shirts off onstage was about saying, *Look, if a guy can take his shirt off, I should be able to take* my *shirt off. Why do my tits have to* mean *something? Because they're a different shape than yours? Why can't I just take my shirt off and be comfortable? It's hot in here!* I mean, I knew perfectly well what it all meant; and then with the rubber dick and getting blowjobs and all that—before I actually identified as a dude, I was already going down that road of fucking with gender.

The *definition* of punk is to subvert the dominant paradigm through art, culture, and music. And we were turning gender on its head, we were turning sexuality on its head, we were turning all these things that had been done in certain way . . . I mean, there were all these dudes in rock 'n' roll with big hair and spandex, or eyeliner or whatever—but they were still like, *We're dudes and we're straight, and we're getting all the babes at the end of the night.* We were *really* fucking with gender. Like, *This is the way we live our lives. And at the end of the night we're going to get the chicks too.*

One thing that happens when I perform is that whatever the performance is that I'm creating, I'm not just creating the performance; *it's creating me.* It's not only the energy loop between me and the audience, it's the energy loop between what I say and what I feel, kind of bouncing back and forth inside me. So I'm like, wow—*I actually* am *a dude. All this acting-out stuff that I'm doing about being a dude is because I'm really a dude!*

And then, the more I talked to dykes at shows and stuff, the more I realized . . . if I said I wanted to lop them off—the twins, the breasticles—they were like, *Nooo!* Especially my girlfriends—*Nooo! I love them! Don't cut them off! I'll throw them in a jar, preserve them in formaldehyde!* Why can't I just have my fucking chest the way I want it? It would be even cooler to be on stage and take my shirt off and *not* have dudes fucking looking at my tits. But I do feel pressure from my old audience about, like, *the breasts!* . . . It's like, *You were looking at my tits the whole fucking time. I told you not to look at my motherfucking tits!* So, whatever. Did they get it? I don't know. On some level I knew that if I took my shirt off people were going to be like, *titties* . . . Everyone loves titties. Even if you suck as a fucking artist and you have some titties, you are going to be popular.

Justin Vivian Bond: There is this whole generation of queer kids now that go to college and have access to documentation of queer history. They have had a kind of a disciplined approach to analyzing and absorbing history

John D'Armour (now known as Hathaway) with just announced presidential candidate Joan Jett Blakk at SPEW II in LA 1992. Photo by Mark Freitas

that no generation of queer people ever had in the past. I am learning so much more from young queer people than I've ever been able to figure out on my own. The language around the issues—I have failings in my own consciousness, in my own habits, and what we used to see as humorous is totally unacceptable now. Things that were painful were turned into jokes, that are now—if you say these jokes you're being transphobic or being racist. It used to be a way for people that were oppressed as trans to joke with each other, like, *Hey, tranny* . . . That word is forbidden now, but I love the word *tranny*. It's a word my girl-friends and I used to recognize each other and make each other comfort-able. It was an umbrella term, like *queer*, for gender variance.

At a certain level I think, *Well, there goes the humor,* but on the other hand it's great that there's a consciousness and conversation around these issues that are elevating it instead of just keeping it in one place— like, *We're trannies and we're oppressed.* There are actually trans people out there saying, *No, we're not, and we refuse to be.* So I don't think it failed at all, I think it's just expanding and becoming more sophisticated, more effective in changing the conversation that allows for people to live dignified lives.

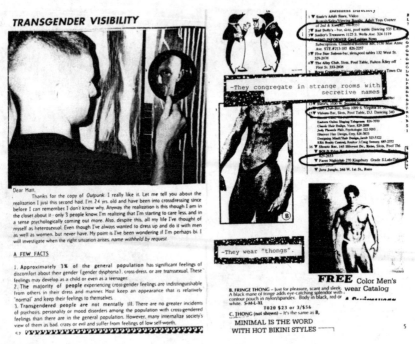

Outpunk no. 3

Penny Arcade: I think about young trans people, and . . . knowing myself, and because I'm still in touch with all the ages I've ever been; if I had been twenty-one in the early '90s, my face would have been tattooed. I was desperate for an identity. So when people go around taking T and cutting off their tits at twenty-two years old, I just feel like somebody should be there saying, *Hey, do you really need to do that* now? *Why don't you wait ten years?*

Trans, to this generation, means transgressive—that they're being transgressive against gender. It just makes me nuts; it's like children in the attic, going through their parents' trunks—like, really? We were just trying to get rid of gender altogether—the idea was that it didn't *matter* what your gender was, that your physical equipment didn't make your gender. People *died* for that. And now things are more gendered than ever! And this younger generation thinks they're being transgressive against gender by totally *reinforcing* the binary thing. I don't know . . .

21

I DON'T WANT WHAT YOU WANT
THOUGHTS ON STYLE

John Waters: I especially loved the girls. I thought that Jordan, who worked in Sex, the shop in London—she was *amazing*. Divine saw Jordan and said, *I feel like Plain Jane* . . . as a matter of fact, that shot of Divine with the Mohawk, from *Female Trouble*, was appropriated for some of the first punk T-shirts, from Sex.

Divine

Punk style seems stronger than hippie style. It's lasted longer. Punk style has never really gone out of fashion—if you see somebody today in full hippie regalia, you think, *Oh boy* . . . But punk still has—this is terrible to say, but it's really a good look for people who aren't so good-looking. For a fat girl, it's the best look ever. That whole Bettie Page look—it's a *great* look, because it makes traditional views of *pretty* or *handsome* just vanish; it doesn't matter, because you're purposely *trying* to make yourself ugly, to regular people. You certainly aren't wearing rings in your nose and everything to make regular people think, *Gee, that looks nice*—you're doing it to set yourself apart from them. Like, *Hey—I don't want what you want*. It's a political fashion that's instantly recognizable.

Divine liked punk from the beginning, because they accepted him right away. Punk boys weren't Divine's type, though. He didn't like 'em skinny. Divine liked porn stars. But I'm sure he got laid in the punk world. Divine got laid a lot, because he just asked everybody, and he wasn't mad if you said no. It's a good way to get through life! A *no* is free.

Cookie: We were rediscovering a lineage—The Slits, Blondie . . . Obviously someone like Poly Styrene influenced my fashion—polka dots, big hair, that sort of thing. For me, queer punk was how I came into my femme identity.

I didn't really know the histories of queer and punk when I was younger. I was going to my first gay rights marches and seeing all these people wearing, like, leather jackets and having shaved heads and bondage gear. I was like, *All these mainstream gay people, wearing all this leather, they think they're so punk but they don't really know what punk is.* I didn't understand the history, which is actually that punk style *came from* gay BDSM culture, motorcycle culture—the leather, studs, and all of that.

Tom Jennings: It's funny, the little things—like my belt, this stupid belt, came from Mr. S Leathers. My god, this belt is old. This belt is like thirty years old. But when we, as punks, would go into Mr. S Leathers to buy a belt, the gay men there did *not* want us in there. They assumed we were straight, which was, of course, wrong. But, also, we just weren't leathermen. It was like, *You're doing it wrong. You're doing our transgression wrong.* No one would ever kick us out of a bar or anything. We just really weren't that welcome and we certainly weren't that interested.

Kembra Pfahler: I was born in Los Angeles, by the beach. And I always felt ostracized just for being born into this body, I always felt that I had to apologize for being my height or my weight or looking the way I did. People would always to tease me about my mouth, my lips, everything. And I'm a contrarian, so I did the complete opposite of what those around me expected, just so that I could maintain my dignity and my sense of self.

When I saw someone like Diamanda Galás doing *Wild Women with Steak Knives* in an evening gown and gigantic hair and extreme eye makeup—when I saw Exene Cervenka onstage with *her* hair, and her strange demeanor—they were creating a standard within themselves that was very challenging, as if they wanted to outdo one another rather than duplicate exactly what the other person was doing. You had people like Phranc, the lesbian folk singer who looked so wildly different from anyone—so completely ahead of her time. So, I was drawn to punk because I felt this shame, and I wanted to overcome it. I wanted to get some *power*. And I like terrifying people with my outfits. You could create your own punk look using availablism; you could come up with your own look very easily, if you had a desire to.

I'm never really naked in my performances. I'm wearing body paint and wigs, and I'm wearing the outfit that I invented for The Voluptuous Horror of Karen Black. I don't know if I'd ever be comfortable just being in my own skin because I love complete transformation. So I never really think of myself as being totally nude, although in the past five years or so I've being going bottomless all the time just because I feel like it looks good. What I wear in The Voluptuous Horror of Karen Black, to me, is just a complicitous outfit that's hard to wear. I made it so that it would be hard to wear, so it would be hard to impostor. You just wouldn't *want* to tape duct tape to your labia or sew your vagina shut. I wanted to do things that would be unbrandable.

Phranc: The image of Phranc evolved out my junior-dyke days. I always wanted to have my brother's haircut, but I was kind of forced to have long hair as a kid. It was soon after I came out and I was living in Venice that I cut my hair. It was way down my back, and I cut it to my shoulders, right before I went on the Lesbian History Exploration, which was a weekend in the Santa Monica mountains with lesbian artists and musicians. While I was there I saw a slideshow by Liza Cowen called *What the Well-Dressed Dyke Will Wear*, which showed all these women in these beautiful suits with these incredible haircuts. Liza had just buzzed all of her hair off, and she looked amazing. So I came home and I went right to the barbershop and just said, *Take it all off.* It was so empowering.

I changed my name on a mountaintop, at this lesbian retreat—I decided I was going to be Franc, with a *C*, like the French franc. And I went to see a friend, I showed up on her doorstep with my new haircut, and said, *I'm Franc!* And she said, *Hold on a minute,* and she went into the other room and came back with a blue baseball cap with the letter P on it. She put in on my head and said, *Phranc! P-h-r-a-n-c.*

Penny Arcade: Quentin Crisp hated music. Quentin said, *Music is the most noise conveying the least amount of information.* But I think that, y'know, certainly he was still living in England during the height of the punk movement there. Quentin was always interested in self-expression, and I think Quentin was very interested in the clothing. He would talk to me about seeing people on St. Mark's Place. During the '90s you would see all these young kids trying to dress, like, '70s punk, like it was 1977—and when *I* see somebody dressed like that it's like seeing Elvis impersonators. Like, *Really? If you're so creative, man, come up with something different!* Quentin would always want to know what the clothing *meant.* Quentin would go crazy when someone was wearing, like, one plaid trouser leg and the other leg leopard print. He'd say, *That's so interesting. What does it* mean? And they'd say, *It doesn't mean anything*—and that would just drive him crazy.

22

"WHERE ARE THEY NOW?"/ WHERE ARE WE NOW?

Hannah Blilie: I was always comfortable with The Gossip being a queer band. I remember being asked quite a few times when *Music for Men* came out whether identifying as a queer band would be, like, ghettoizing ourselves. And I was like—first of all, that's a fucking weird question. It's who we are; it's our identity. I don't *care* if people are uncomfortable with that. And yes, if we can break it into the mainstream, great!—but we're not going to stop saying that we're lesbians. Those are our roots, that's our community and that's where we feel most comfortable. So no, I don't feel like I'm *ghettoizing* myself or limiting myself. That question always stuck with me. I just had a reaction like, *No! I don't give a shit!*

Bruce Benderson: I don't think that sexuality or sexual orientation is enough to create an entire culture around. If you go to sex parties that straight people don't go to, it means your sexuality is different; it doesn't mean that your entire identity or your entire lifestyle is different. The only culture that exists around sexuality in Western culture at the moment is marriage and the family. It's no coincidence that so many gays are interested in gay marriage and adoption issues, because they can't find a complete cultural lifestyle anywhere else. When I was younger, I went to the most extreme sexual environments you can imagine for my pleasure. And who would I see? People who worked in publishing, lawyers, actors, delivery boys. They had a sexual urge that they wanted to satisfy, and that was the only thing that made them like me. I don't care whether it's called homocore or queercore; I don't believe it's a culture, I don't believe it's a world. Unless you're sexually obsessed. If you're sexually obsessed that's your world, but I don't think queer is a word for it. Maybe the word for it is addictive personality.

Oppression and the response to that oppression created an underground culture, a culture of denial and resistance—but there's very little need for that anymore! You don't have to hide the fact that you're gay, and if you tell your middle-class family that you're gay, they're going to embrace it. Gay culture was a culture of oppression, and as soon as that oppression was lifted more and more that culture disappeared like a dream. It's the same as happens to any minority; when you lift the restrictions against them there is no way for them to go but into mainstream life and they are absorbed and corrupted by it. It's true of black people, it's true of gay people, it's true of anybody. Sodomy is no longer against the law. You won't be sent to a mental institution for shock treatment. You're just somebody who likes to fuck people of the same sex—you could be anything. And I feel the same way about *queer art*, I don't think there is such thing as queer art unless it deals bleakly with sexuality, and then I would call it sexual art or erotic art. I don't think that just because a person is gay and creates art, that *queer art* been created.

Brontez Purnell: There's plenty of white queer kids that I know that think just because they're queer it puts their experience right on par with everything the kids in Selma were doing, the kids in Germany in the 1930s were doing . . . but I don't think that's necessarily true. I think radicalism is a very individualized, personal revolution. I hope that people have enough self-awareness that just because you call yourself queer, it doesn't give you this pass. Sometimes people call themselves queer to give themselves this kind of pass. I don't think that that's always true. I've seen a lot of kind of fuck-escapism, people just being like, *Oh, I'm queer, so I'm just like all these other historical figures that have had oppression*. But every other person I've seen that calls themselves queer, I'm just like, *No, you're not actually on par with all these people*. That's not going to give you a pass, actually. In fact, some of y'all are even fucking worse, actually.

Adam Rathe: Y'know, the times have changed. We're living in a time where people who grow up with Team Dresch posters on their walls now work at mainstream magazines. There's an entire generation of people that were influenced by this who are now kind of feeding information back. I think attitudes have changed. I think that twenty years on, people can see the impact in ways that might not been able to see at the time. I think that hopefully people are interested in righting some of the mistakes that were made. If it was ignored when it was happening, we can't change that, but we can talk about it *now* and try to make sure people don't forget. And I think that we're also at a point where that sort of culture—the culture of written word, people taking road trips to random cities to see one another, to play in bands, to put together zines, to do whatever—doesn't happen as often. People living online kind of saps some of the vitality out of it.

If Peaches wants to call herself queercore, if someone wants to keep that word alive, I think that's fantastic. I don't think anyone wants put boundaries on who uses the word or why. Liz Naylor famously said something like, *Queercore wasn't a movement, it was a moment*; so I think the only reaction that a modern band calling themselves queercore might get is that it's a little *retro*. I can't imagine many bands today referring to themselves as riot grrrl either—not because the ideals of riot grrrl aren't important or because they don't believe in them, but because the terminology seems a little bit passé.

But if it still matters to someone, it still exists. I do think that queercore started to sputter out; I mean, there wasn't some great implosion where everyone turned in the membership cards. After the Dirtybird festival, after Homo A Gogo, I think it started to feel watered down to some people who were originally part of the scene. But for others, the doors were just opening; if you're a kid going to Homo A Gogo, you might not *care* about the SPEW conference in Chicago that happened a hundred years before—it wasn't relevant to you. So . . . I don't know if really disappeared so much as it spread out.

Tom Jennings: We used to do things like write letters, which is really weird to do now. Like, actually writing something and putting in an envelope and putting a stamp on it. And the response time—once you sent it out, it would take three days to get there, three days to get around to reading it, a week to write a response—that was an acceptable turnaround time. Now you go, *Oh my god*—you can't even imagine.

Genesis P-Orridge: People's experiences in life are being reduced daily. In the 1960s, when we wanted to find a book about William Burroughs, we would have to go through this whole ritual . . . lying to my parents about where we're going to be—I'd say, *I'm going to visit my friend's* *grandparents in the suburbs in London for the weekend, but we'll be safe—* and then getting money for the train from my parents, then hitchhiking to London to keep the money. And hitchhiking, you meet four or five people that you would never otherwise meet. And some of them have really interesting lives to talk about. Then you arrive in London with no place to stay, and you have to walk around and find somebody who you think might let you sleep on their floor; usually, in those days, they had long hair. And then the next day you would walk around Soho, because the only books by Jean Genet, Henry Miller, Burroughs, and so on were all in porno shops. So you would see all this underground sexual culture that normally is hidden. And eventually, after finding a book, you do the whole thing in reverse to get back home. Now, you go to Amazon and click. The amount of richness and experience and lost information that happens by just going *click* is tragic. And we talk to younger people that grew up with the internet and . . . they don't get it. *But I still read the book.* Yes, you read the book, but what about the *book of life*?

G.B. Jones: When I read people's theses, y'know—when a university student is doing their PhD, they're doing their thesis on *J.D.s* and queercore or they're doing their thesis on riot grrrl, and they have all these criticisms—I would just like to say to these people, our zines weren't directed at university students doing their theses; they were directed at our own community. And when I read about people criticizing, like, three eighteen-year-old girls doing fanzines out of their bedrooms, like the riot grrrls, I think, y'know, they didn't really have the backing of a large institution, like whatever your university is, to put out a call for papers across the internet—because there was no internet then—and cherry-pick from the best applicants. They had to go with who lived next door, who played at their local club, and what they could make of that, just the way we did. We had to go with friends who worked at the same restaurant we did or the same bar. Or hung out at Together's.

Johnny Noxzema: God, it's laughable—you Google "queercore" and you see all this crap, people writing these ridiculous essays. At least go to the Archives and look at the actual fanzines. Most of these things, they take a couple of quotes that have been already regurgitated by somebody else. They haven't even seen what they're writing about! How can you defend a thesis on something that you haven't even seen?

Deke Nihilson: Punk's not dead, is just smells like it is. No, actually I'm really struck by the resilience of punk, as a set of social tools for kids who otherwise don't fit in. It's an idea that just won't die, which is amazing; it really is. And it's gone on to have immense cultural influence, and yet remains its own thing, and I think that's great. A lot of punks get down on this idea of *selling out* or whatever. But I think that kind of ability to sway popular consciousness among masses of people is exactly what anarchists lost track of. And I think it's delightful that punk has—there are punk operas on Broadway. It's amazing, that's just utterly amazing. And I say more power to 'em.

SMASHING ORTHODOXIES
BY WALTER CRASSHOLE

There shouldn't be an epilogue or final word on a movement like queer-core. That would imply that it's over. But something like queercore can barely be contained by the word. It's too wild and big and frenetic to be finished. Its disparate elements can hardly be defined, and if it can't be defined, it can't be pinned down. Queercore can live on in yet-to-be determined forms.

Even for the editors of the book, queercore is difficult or impossible to pin down. For me, a teenager growing up in Alaska at the end of the of the 1990s and early 2000s, *punk* came before *queer*. But growing up in a far-flung, provincial part of the US, I didn't have much of a choice—it was one allegiance or none. I didn't even consider the idea that choosing both (or more) was possible. As I began understanding the homo within and intertwining that with my punk identity, it totally seemed like a natural fit, but it had to occur to me first. When I first saw Bruce LaBruce's *The Raspberry Reich* at the Castro Theatre in San Francisco in 2004, it fucked me up the ass—hard. These were punks doing some seri-ously queer shit with fucking bravado. "They're out there," I thought. I may not have been able to define it, but at that moment an unnamed fusion of queer and punk energies seemed like the most important thing in the world—not something that belonged in the past, although most of this book takes place before that movie was released. Undefined then, but totally worth exploring, even now.

What kind of movement is queercore? It is in many ways a descend-ent of the LGBTIQ* rights movements that came before it—traces of these movements are embedded in its DNA. Gay rights movement(s) had been ebbing and flowing in some form since the early twentieth century: first in Germany, then in other parts of the world until bursting forth during the social and cultural upheaval of the 1960s—ignited in colorful fury on the fiery night of the Stonewall riots on June 28, 1969, when Marsha P. Johnson and Sylvia Rivera (two QPOC sex workers) led the patrons of the Stonewall Inn in New York against a marauding NYPD. The original gay rights movement manifested itself in radical groups like New York's Gay Liberation Front and later San Francisco's Lavender Panthers.

The late 1970s saw the first pleas for assimilation and the rise of the Gay Clone. By then, gay liberation had seemingly shifted much of its focus to issues of acceptance and assimilation. Sure, there was a lot going on beneath the surface: Harry Hays founded the Radical Faeries in 1978, and radical lesbians were calling for separatist strategies. But as the 1980s began, amid a new wave of conservatism, the younger queer generation felt that much was lacking. Perhaps punk rock could give the gay movement the kick in the ass it needed. And as with many movements in the twentieth century, you had to look to the kids to find it.

To call it a youth movement would be short-sighted, considering the age range and period(s) queercore encompassed—but the energy and ferocity of its filmmakers, writers, musicians, and artists certainly made it look that way. Some of its protagonists were young when it started. It might be described as a youth attitude. But many of the queerdos in this book are still putting out work with an antiestablishment sneer. Lynn Breedlove is currently working with his band Commando and helming Homobiles, a ride service to get nightlife performers and the LGBTQIA community safely to and fro. In December of 2019, Justin Vivian Bond performed in Olga Neuwirth's staging of Virginia Woolf's *Orlando*, the first-ever production in the Vienna State Opera House by a woman. And, of course, Bruce LaBruce has never stopped making films throughout the years, oscillating between cinematic hardcore pornography and more "traditional" films that still get festival attention, however far from mainstream they are. None of these people are close to their twenties, but all are putting out challenging work at a breakneck pace. And there's always an infusion of fresh blood to keep queercore young in age: Against Me! and their transgender lead singer and founder Laura Jane Grace have a huge presence as new faces of queer punk rock for another generation of kids.

Many have called queercore a political or sociopolitical movement, and that's explored pretty extensively in the book. Queercore has certainly inspired continued direct political action well into the new millennium. The Gay Shame movement, for instance, which originated in late-90s New York, protested assimilation and the crass commercialization of gay pride by holding counterpride parades throughout the 2000s. But queercore has always resisted orthodoxies—there has never been a ten-point political platform.

Is it a cultural movement? All those records, films and zines probably left a bigger mark on the queer scene (and the larger world) than anything else. They were what really inspired isolated queer folks to pick up that guitar or sewing machine, or start using photocopiers or writing blogs. By the noughties, artists inspired by queercore had made significant cracks in the mainstream, with albums like Peaches's *The Teaches of Peaches* in 2000, and The Gossip's 2004 breakthrough soul-dance-punk amalgam *Standing in the Way of Control*. There's an almost unscalable mountain of cultural artifacts that queercore left behind. And they keep coming—fierce new bands like the all-black/femme Fuck U Pay Us, who opened for Bikini Kill on their recent reunion tour (more on that later).

The impact of this blast of queer culture was apparent to both Yony Leyser and myself when we arrived in Berlin in the early 2010s. We landed right in the middle of another queer punk explosion—not one aping what had come before in the US or Canada or the UK but one existing on its own terms. Parties like Rattenbar, occupied houses like Köpi and its Queer Gala nights, and bars like Silver Future spawned long nights of sex, politics, and creative hedonism. Yony Leyser and I met through this scene, introduced through a filmmaker and mutual friend. I was working as an English-language queer journalist, and Yony was just sowing the seeds of his *Queercore* documentary—and getting me involved. Queercore was still vital in numerous ways.

Queercore is many diverse movements joyously clusterfucked into one—not fitting into any neat category but inspiring generations of artists and activists. So, what about today? Does the world still need queercore or a movement like it? Does it matter? Or are the issues that queercore dealt with over and settled? When we conducted the original interviews, obviously no one could imagine the position we would be in in the coming years. The election of Donald Trump in 2016 proved a weighty counterbalance to any notion of continued progress. One of Trump's first acts as president was to remove any mention of LGBT issues from the White House web-site—a dog whistle letting his constituents know what the priorities would be in this new radical right-wing era. Over the following years, he undermined trans* positions in the military and championed archaic gender enforcement laws in public bathrooms, humiliating and endangering trans* people across of the US. His message was explicit: trans* people do not deserve the same protections as everyone else. Ironically, in the years leading up to Trump, we seemed to get everything we *weren't* fighting for—including gay marriage and the abovementioned trans* military presence. Much of

No Skin off My Ass

this is said and done. To push back against gay marriage now seems painfully regressive or at least a misdirected use of energy. Queercore may not have fought for any of this stuff, but we got it anyway.

Along with the legalization of gay marriage came a mainstream-ing of queer culture. A trans* black woman became one of the most beloved characters on the women-in-prison dramedy *Orange Is the New Black*—paving the way for the largely trans, POC television show *Pose* a few years down the line. RuPaul brought drag culture to the mainstream with her immensely successful reality show *RuPaul's Drag Race* and is now a household name. Chelsea Manning became a hero for leaking nearly 750,000 classified US military documents to the whistleblower platform WikiLeaks. After her identity was made public, she came out as trans* to the world. Manning was jailed for the document leak, but little public noise was made about her gender identity. In some ways, and some specific cases, queer people were making headway. In other ways, it was pure distraction.

Even queercore has seen its share of mainstreaming. In early 2020, Vaginal Davis was invited to show her 1999 film *The White to Be Angry* at the historic Art Institute of Chicago. Carrie Brownstein may be just as well known for her hit comedy sketch series *Portlandia* as she is for her band Sleater-Kinney. And Tribe 8 guitarist Silas Howard has had a major impact on the mainstream as the first trans director of the hit show *Transparent*. The freaks and geeks of yesteryear have gone beyond the vilified vanguard to become respected voices in prestige media and art. What does this heightened visibility of fringe queers mean? Have we landed in a radical new queer utopia because a few have broken through?

During the 2020 US Democratic primaries, one of the leading candidates was small-town Indiana mayor Pete Buttigieg—a white, educated, former military man just middle-of-the-road enough to not upset most of the Democratic Party. Buttigieg's positions were far from progressive, and aside from being openly gay (and noticeably younger than the other candidates), he didn't particularly stand out. But even as Buttigieg came closer to the White House than any openly gay candidate before him, many queers kicked up quite a fuss, throwing their weight behind the further-left (and straight) senator Bernie Sanders . . . proving that gay still doesn't sing to us all the same way. Many saw Pete Buttigieg as a mere pinkwashing of a neoliberal agenda from the center-left—more of the systemic same wrapped in a rainbow flag.

But back to the state of the larger world: it's not just the US but the planet in general that has made a dangerous pivot to the right. In the UK there was Brexit; Austria up until very recently had a ruling government with a far-right party in its coalition; and Russia, Poland, Brazil, the Philippines, India, Hungary, Israel, and Holland have all exhibited extreme-right tendencies as of late. While most of these right-wing upswings were rooted in xenophobia, history has shown that queers are always somewhere on that target list. Russia's offenses were catapulted into the spotlight with the arrest of Pussy Riot in 2012 for their storming of a cathedral in Moscow. Russia then expanded its oppression of minorities with their Gay Propaganda Law and through Putin's blind eye to the massacre of LGBT people in the southern region of Chechnya. This institutionalized homophobia and LGBTIQ* terror extends all the way to the western parts of the former Communist Bloc, as more than a hundred different Polish municipalities have declared themselves to be "LGBT Free Zones," denouncing the western "import" of homosexuality.

Maybe it's this blend of radical right-wing populism and a tepid response from the (gay and straight) Left establishment that has made the ground so fertile for the reemergence of queercore-aligned artists and bands. By 2015, female-fronted rock bands of the 1990s were having a full-fledged renaissance, to varying degrees of success: kicked off by a botched Babes in Toyland regrouping, followed by Sleater-Kinney and finally, to perhaps the biggest fanfare, Bikini Kill in 2019. Dyke-core legends Team Dresch also reunited to huge excitement. None of these bands were mere legacy acts—this wasn't Jerry Only dragging the corpse of The Misfits through dive bars across America for a bit of cash. Back in 2015, with #metoo making its first noise, there was a genuine need for these voices to reemerge. Whether it was conscious or serendipitous, who knows? Either way, it was remarkable to see the issues that these bands had sung so loudly about in the 1990s only now being taken seriously on a broader scale. And fans and bands alike seem to be genuinely elated to be reconnecting with one another. Queercore can do this too.

While the roots covered in this book begin in 1969, queercore's expiration date has yet to be declared. There are still so many reasons to fight. The original pioneers are still here—making music, film, art, literature, politics, whatever—and there's certainly room for younger voices to join in. The adage in punk is to rip it up and start again. And if you want to do that, go ahead. Rip it, shred it, burn it, whatever. But don't forget it. Be whatever it takes to shake some shit up in all-too-straight world. It still needs it.

GLOSSARY OF PROTAGONISTS

Penny Arcade: Queer performance artist who first rose to prominence during Warhol's Factory time. Has worked with everyone from Paul Morrissey to Quentin Crisp.

Tony Arena: New York artist, filmmaker, and musician behind illustrated gay punk romance comic *Anonymous Boy*, which first appeared in *J.D.s*. Also went on to illustrate record art for Pansy Division, Limp Wrist, and more.

Glenn Belverio: Journalist and editor of zine *Pussy Grazer*. Video artist and political activist under the guise of Glennda Orgasm. Did performance art with the likes of Camille Paglia and Bruce LaBruce.

Bruce Benderson: One of the great contemporary homosexual writers and essayists and general champion of degeneracy. Renowned for his 1994 novel about a black street hustler, *User*.

Jody Bleyle: Founding member, singer, and guitarist for groundbreaking dyke-core outfit Team Dresch. Founder of queercore label Candy Ass Records, the label behind the 1995 women's self-defense record *Free to Fight*. Still makes music and occasionally tours with Team Dresch.

Hannah Blilie: Second drummer of the most commercially successful queercore band The Gossip, first appearing on breakthrough record *Standing in the Way of Control*. The Gossip called it quits in 2016, but Blilie continues to make music.

Mykel Board: Journalist and longtime columnist for *Maximum Rocknroll*. Famously wrote often about his bisexuality and being punk.

Don Bolles: Drummer for prolific punk bands The Germs and 45 Grave in the late 1970s/early 1980s Los Angeles and coauthor of 2002's *Lexicon Devil: The Fast Times and Short Life of Darby Crash and the Germs*.

Justin Vivian Bond: Trans activist, artist, and performance artist based in New York City and one half of the famous performance duo Kiki & Herb. Bond was also at the 1988 San Francisco Gay Pride with the cop float and visible standing atop the "police" car with other queer punks.

Lynn Breedlove: Founding member of hardcore/punk queercore band Tribe 8, known for explicit lyrics and provocative stage shows that included slicing strap-on dildos off and boys on leashes. Breedlove is also the author of punk tome *Godspeed* and continues to have an influential writing career.

Joanna Brown: Cofounder, along with Mark Freitas, of Homocore Chicago in 1992. Responsible for connecting much of the queercore scene in other areas to the Midwest. Also involved in SPEW: The Homographic Convergence—a queer zine convention—in 1991.

Jena von Brucker: Member of original queercore scene in Toronto and contributor to *J.D.s*. In part responsible for fabricating the whole original queercore scene. Part of infamous William S. Burroughs takedown zine *Double Bill*.

Jürgen Brüning: Berlin-based producer behind many of Bruce LaBruce's films—starting with *No Skin off My Ass*. Brüning continues to produce experimental and provocative queer cinema and founded the Pornfilmfestival Berlin in 2006.

Dennis Cooper: Novelist and poet as well as art critic for publications such as *Art in America*, editor at *Artforum*, and generally responsible for getting queercore artists' names out to the general public. His books themselves qualify him well enough as a queercore figure, most prominently the five fiction novels that make up the famously graphic *George Miles Cycle*.

Jayne County: First openly transgender rock and punk icon, musician, actor, and artist, known for protopunk band Wayne/Jayne County and The Electric Chairs.

Vaginal Davis: Iconic black drag queen, performance artist, and actor of the queercore scene. Collaborated with many from Glenn Meadmore to Bruce LaBruce, as well as editor of zine *Fertile La Toyah Jackson*. Also behind bands PME, Black Fag, and Cholita. Originally based in LA, she's lived in Berlin since 2006.

Donna Dresch: The namesake, singer, and guitarist behind seminal Olympia, Washington, dyke and queercore band Team Dresch, she is also the woman behind record label Chainsaw Records, which released early recordings from Sleater-Kinney among others. She was also on the cover of issue 5 of *Homocore* fanzine.

Scott Free: Award-winning queer singer-songwriter based in Chicago. Hosts the twice-monthly queer performance night Homolatte, the longest-running queer performance night in the US.

Mark Freitas: Cofounded Homocore Chicago with Joanna Brown in 1992 and ran it until its end in 2001.

Jon Ginoli: Lead singer and guitarist of the San Francisco band that brought queercore to the pop-punk mainstream—Pansy Division. With explicitly gay lyrics and record art, they delivered homosexuality to the suburban masses, whether they liked it or not.

Kim Gordon: Cofounder, bassist, and singer for New York City alt/noise rock outfit Sonic Youth and an outspoken voice for women in music. The band helped introduce much of alternative rock to the wider world, including bands like Nirvana but also underground acts like Bikini Kill.

Brian Grillo: Openly gay and HIV-positive singer of alt-rock outfit Extra Fancy (1992–1997). One of the few bands with an openly gay frontperson to get a major-label record deal, they were quickly dropped— it's rumored precisely because of the band's openness about Grillo's sexuality.

Kathleen Hanna: Musician, singer, and writer best known for riot grrrl band Bikini Kill and electro-dance outfit Le Tigre. Hanna, among others, was also behind the early 1990s riot grrrl movement, queercore's feminism-centered contemporary punk movement, kicking off new feminist involvement for the late-twentieth century and beyond.

Silas Howard: Guitarist for dyke and queercore band Tribe 8. In 2001 his queer buddy film *By Hook or by Crook*, premiered at Sundance. He has also recently directed episodes of the award-winning series *Transparent*.

Tom Jennings: Copublisher of San Francisco's *Homocore* zine from 1988 to 1991, which was immeasurably important to the queercore scene. Jennings also organized homocore shows, bringing traditionally "straight" bands like Fugazi into the scene. Works today as a technician at the University of California, Irvine.

G.B. Jones: Toronto-based coeditor of the zine that "started it all," *J.D.s*, along with Bruce LaBruce. Drummer for all-dyke queercore outfit Fifth Column. Director of 2008's *The Lollipop Generation*.

Bruce LaBruce: Along with G.B. Jones, considered one of the godparents of Queercore. Started out as go-go boy for G.B.'s band Fifth Column, then coedited legendary queercore zine *J.D.s.* Went on to become quite the director. Look it up.

Larry Livermore: Put the Northern California East Bay scene on the map through the label he cofounded, Lookout! Records—responsible for, among others, Pansy Division and Green Day. Contributor to *Homocore*.

Mads Ananda Lodahl: Danish queer activist, writer, and lecturer. Founded underground group Queer Jihad in 2005 and in 2006 cofounded the now-defunct annual Copenhagen Queer Festival. His book *Inappropriate Behavior*—a book of essays on gender and sexuality—came out in 2018.

Sara Marcus: Author of the definitive word on the riot grrrl movement, *Girls to the Front: The True Story of the Riot Grrrl Revolution*, published in 2010.

Andrew Martini: Bassist and cofounder of Limp Wrist, *the* premiere faggot punk rock band of the 2000s. Based in New York City, he still makes music and tours with Limp Wrist, their latest release being 2017's *Facades*.

Billy Miller: Editor of what could be considered one of the world's first queer zines, *Straight to Hell a.k.a. The Manhattan Review of Unnatural Acts*, since 1971. *STH* was one of the first ways for gay men to get subversive gay erotica in the US. New issues of *STH* still occasionally come out.

Milo Miller: Cofounder of the Queer Zine Archive Project, or QZAP, in 2003—a living, online archive of DIY publications made by queers.

Eileen Myles: American author, poet, and activist punk. Author of her own cult autobiographical novel *Chelsea Girls* and presidential candidate in 1992 on the platform "openly female."

Deke Nihilson: Coeditor of San Francisco's influential *Homocore* zine (1988-1991), which included contributions from G.B. Jones, Larry Livermore, Donna Dresch, and more. Currently a filmmaker residing in Portland, Oregon.

Johnny Noxzema: Along with Rex Ray, coedited Toronto-based zine *Bimbox*. When LaBruce and G.B. Jones split, Noxzema contributed to the infamous *Double Bill* zine as well.

Kembra Pfahler: Lead singer and founder of punk group The Voluptuous Horror of Karen Black and known for her outrageous stage performance with giant wigs and full body paint. Modeled and acted in the late 1980s/early 1990s, including in Richard Kern's *Sewing Circle*.

Phranc: The self-described "all-American Jewish lesbian folk singer" who got her start in several prolific and queer early Los Angeles punk bands including Catholic Discipline and Nervous Gender.

Genesis Breyer P-Orridge: Queer icon and third-gender cofounder of industrial pioneers Throbbing Gristle and experimental post-punk group Psychic TV. Founded magical order Thee Temple ov Psychick Youth in 1981 and embarked on a pandrogyny project with Lady Jaye Breyer P-Orridge in the 2000s in which the two surgically transformed themselves into each other.

Brontez Purnell: Former member of queer punk-rap act Gravy Train!!!, frontman of his own project The Younger Lovers, and author of books *Johnny Would You Love Me If My Dick Were Bigger* and *Since I Lay My Burden Down*, director of *Unstoppable Feat: The Dances of Ed Mock* and *100 Boyfriends Mixtape*. Currently lives in Oakland.

Adam Rathe: Journalist and writer for mainstream LGBT publication *OUT* and wrote "Queer to the Core," a mini-oral history of queercore in 2012.

Larry-Bob Roberts: San Francisco–based publisher of queer zine (print and online) *Holy Tit Clamps* since 1989, author of *The International Homosexual Conspiracy* and commentator on queer culture past and present.

Sarah Schulman: Academic early activist with ACT UP. Cofounder of New York Gay and Lesbian Experimental Film Festival, MIX, in 1987 and author of books like *Gentrification of the Mind* and *Conflict Is Not Abuse*. Cowrote—with New Queer Cinema pioneer Cheryl Dunye—*The Owls* and *Mommy Is Coming*, the latter of which was produced by Bruce LaBruce's longtime producer Jürgen Brüning.

Martín Sorrondeguy: San Francisco–based singer for Latino-hardcore band Los Crudos and queercore hardcore punk band Limp Wrist and behind DIY indie label Lengua Armada. Was also a huge figure in the straight edge scene.

Anna Joy Springer: One of three singers of the epic 924 Gilman St. scene punk band Blatz, then a singer in Blatz "country" offshoot The Gr'ups, followed by all-dyke queercore band Cypher in the Snow. Anna Joy went on to tour with San Francisco–based lesbian-feminist spoken-word and performance art collective Sister Spit and became a published author of books like *The Birdwisher* (2009) and *The Vicious Red Relic, Love* (2011).

Tantrum: Bassist for confrontational dyke-core and queercore band Tribe 8.

Scott Treleaven: Gay artist, zine publisher, and filmmaker best known for his 1990s zine *This Is the Salivation Army* and the first queercore documentary in 1996, *Queercore: A Punk-u-mentary*—as much an artifact of the scene as it is a document of it.

Ed Varga: Trans activist punk organizer with Homocore Minneapolis and later founded the Homo A Gogo festival in Olympia in 2002, which moved to San Francisco in 2009.

John Waters: Legendary cult filmmaker/director behind films like *Pink Flamingos, Female Trouble, Hairspray*, and many more.

Chris Wilde: Photographer and cofounder of the Queer Zine Archive Project with Milo Miller in 2003.

Kaia Wilson: Vocalist, guitarist, and founder of both Team Dresch in the 1990s and The Butchies in the 2000s, in addition to operating Mr. Lady Records, which put out records by Le Tigre and Electrelane, among others.

Cookie Woolner: Drummer for SF all-women goth-punk band Subtonix, now a PhD in history and women's studies who wrote her dissertation on African American women and same-sex desire.

A QUEERCORE AND QUEERCORE-INFLUENTIAL FILMOGRAPHY

The Decline of Western Civilization, **1981, D: Penelope Spheeris** The legendary documentary survey of the early LA punk scene, featuring interviews and live performances of bands like X and Black Flag, as well as queer figures like Darby Crash of the Germs, Phranc (as part of Catholic Discipline), and Alice Bag.

Female Trouble, **1974, D: John Waters** The underground cult smash follow-up to Waters's *Pink Flamingos*, starring drag superstar Divine as Dawn Davenport, a juvenile delinquent sent on the path of crime when she didn't get her cha-cha heels for Christmas. *Female Trouble* was a major inspiration on punk and queer ethos and style.

Fingered, **1986, D: Richard Kern** Perhaps the most famous film to come out of the Cinema of Transgression—a dirty, confrontational Super 8 film movement that came from the 1980s New York no wave scene—*Fingered* features no wave icons Lydia Lunch and Lung Leg. Controversial for its time, its portrayal of brutal, violent, and explicit sexual situations—a rape scene with a gun, among others—would be considered even more taboo today.

Green Pubes, **1995, D: Anonymous Boy** Tony Arena's low-budget animated short is everything a boy-meets-boy punk film should be: loud, low-fi, sexy, and raucous. It had some success on the film festival circuit.

A Gun for Jennifer, **1997, D: Todd Morris** An entry in the rape and revenge b-movie genre, *A Gun* is most notable for an extended concert scene featuring dyke-core band Tribe 8—dildo castration and all.

Hustler White, **1996, D: Bruce LaBruce, Rick Castro** A sexually explicit homage to Billy Wilder's 1950 Hollywood tragedy *Sunset Boulevard*, LaBruce and Castro's *Hustler White* dives into the world of the Santa Monica Boulevard hustler with model and one-time Madonna boyfriend Tony Ward as its lead. Vaginal Davis and queer performance artist Glen Meadmore also make appearances. This was the only collaboration LaBruce did with Castro.

It Changed My Life: Bikini Kill in the UK, **1993, D: Lucy Thane** One of the few ways to see Bikini Kill, and riot grrrl in general, on their own terms. Hanna and the band were notoriously anti-press at the time, and Thane delivers a look into the world of the young band in their beginnings.

Jubilee, **1978, D: Derek Jarman** Queer director Jarman's punk dystopia film may have predated queercore by a few years but the collision of the two sensibilities were the closest thing the genre has to its own "classic." Features appearances by Jayne County, The Slits, Adam and the Ants, and a lot of English sneering.

L.A. Zombie, **2010, D: Bruce LaBruce** LaBruce returns to LA with a hardcore zombie porno starring French porno legend François Sagat. The film was banned from the Melbourne International Film Festival by Australian censors after initially being accepted. Also features Tony Ward.

Liquid Sky, **1982, D: Slava Tsukerman** The New York–set new wave sci-fi film was just as responsible for the aesthetics of art-damaged punk as it was influential for being an androgynous, gender-bending, underground cult hit.

The Lollipop Generation, **2008, D: G.B. Jones** G.B. Jones's first feature length film shot over fifteen years on Super 8. It features a cross-section of queercore icons including Vaginal Davis, Jena von Brucker, K Records's Calvin Johnson, Joel Gibb of Hidden Cameras, Johnny Noxzema, and Anonymous Boy.

My Father Is Coming, **1991, D: Monika Treut** The fourth feature film by the celebrated German lesbian filmmaker, cowritten with gay cult author Bruce Benderson, follows the exploits of a German actor in the US trying to conceal her failures from her visiting father and features porn actor, activist, and writer Annie Sprinkle.

No Skin off My Ass, **1991, D: Bruce LaBruce** The film the catapulted LaBruce into the public spotlight and made him an international cult sensation. Kurt Cobain once called the low-budget black-and-white tale of a faggy hairdresser and a skinhead who fall in love his favorite film. Cowritten with G.B. Jones but uncredited, the film's success sparked the rift between LaBruce and Jones and thus the scene itself.

Pink Flamingos, **1972, D: John Waters** Waters's breakthrough film starring Divine as the "filthiest person alive" is arguably the mother of all
underground films, with its outrageous dialog and images—including
Divine eating real dog shit—put Waters in the international spotlight.

The Raspberry Reich, **2004, D: Bruce LaBruce** LaBruce takes on Germany's
infamous 1970s left-wing terrorist cell the Baader-Meinhof Gang in
his hardcore gay porn take on a gang of radical revolutionaries that
claim "heterosexuality is the opiate of the masses." Susanne Sachsse
stars as their fearless leader, and Genesis P-Orridge makes a cameo as
a TV announcer.

Queercore, **1996, D: Scott Trelevan** The original documentary on queercore. At just twenty minutes, it's a short blast of firsthand documentation of the queercore scene in the 1990s by the man behind *This Is
the Salivation Army*.

She's Real, **1997, D: Lucy Thane** Thane's contribution to 1990s documentary exploration of queercore, this one focusing mostly on dyke and
women* protagonists (Phranc, Donna Dresch, G.B. Jones, et al.), as
well as Jody Bleyle's Candy Ass Records and the *Free to Fight* compilation album, a project about women's self-defense.

Super 8½, **1994, D: Bruce LaBruce** LaBruce's follow-up to *No Skin off My
Ass* is a smorgasbord of cinematic homage, as well as a send-up to the
relationship between G.B. Jones and LaBruce. It stars LaBruce himself
as a failing porn star and features appearances by Scott Thompson as
Buddy Cole, Vaginal Davis, Richard Kern, and Ben Weasel of Screeching
Weasel.

The Troublemakers, **1990, D: G.B. Jones** One of G.B. Jones earliest Super
8 shorts and queercore films featuring Toronto scenesters Bruce
LaBruce, Caroline Azar, and Jo the Ho.

*What Is the Relationship between Rosa Von Praunheim and the Male Strippers
in San Francisco?*, **1990, D: Jürgen Brüning, Mark Goldstein** Bruce
LaBruce's longtime producer juxtaposes German gay liberation icon
(and filmmaker in his own right) Rosa von Praunheim with the male
sex workers of the Bay Area to investigate the question: Why were
there no openly gay mainstream directors in the US and no go-go boys
in Germany in 1990?

The YoYo Gang, **1992, D: G.B. Jones** Jones's dyke-centric follow-up exploita-
tion short to *The Troublemakers*, this one featuring a primarily lesbian
cast including many big queercore names like Donna Dresch of Team

Dresch, Leslie Mah of Tribe 8, and Caroline Azar of Fifth Column, as well as Bruce LaBruce and *Homocore* editor Deke Nihilson.

SELECTED CINEMATIC SOMEBODIES

Kenneth Anger Author of 1959 cult gossip pseudo-exposé *Hollywood Babylon*, but much more well known for his underground experimental film work which including *Invocation of My Demon Brother*, *Lucifer Rising*, and 1963's initially banned *Scorpio Rising*, which included homosexual, leather, and Nazi imagery set to the pop music of the era.

Peter de Rome British writer, photographer, and filmmaker known as the "Grandfather of Gay Porn" for his critically acclaimed short films he began making in the 1960s. Many were collected in *The Erotic Films of Peter de Rome*.

Jean Genet The French gay writer, philosopher, and activist always favored the marginalized elements of society from petty criminals to homosexuals, which he considered the same milieu. Genet's work was prolific and included his only foray into film, *Un Chant d'Amour*, a black-and-white underground short about the homosexual fantasies of a prison inmate.

Fred Halsted One of the most celebrated pornographers of the gay porn's 1960s–70s halcyon days, the LA filmmakers' classics *Sex Garage* and *L.A. Plays Itself* are the only gay pornos in the permanent collection of the Museum of Modern Art.

Barbara Hammer A pioneer of lesbian filmmaking, Hammer's film were cutting-edge in the 1970s, showing explicit representations of lesbian sexuality from a female gaze and continued to be experimental through her whole career—by her own admission, if the way she lived was an experiment, her art should be too.

Kuchar Brothers Twin brothers George and Mike Kucher came out of the same underground cinema generation as Warhol, Anger, and Stan Brakhage, much of their output having a homoerotic aspect to it. George died in 2011 in San Francisco.

Curt McDowell Director of the underground pornographic (homo- and heterosexual) cult classic *Thunder Crack*, written by George Kuchar of the Kuchar Brothers. This 1975 low-budget black comedy sits alongside John Waters's early work as the best in underground cinema.

Paul Morrissey American underground filmmaker whose films were often confused with Andy Warhol, while many had Warhol's name (as producer) over the title. Best known for his trilogy with Warhol pretty boy and underground icon Joe Dallesandro (*Flesh* [1968], *Trash* [1970], *Heat* [1972]) and his 1970s adaptations of *Dracula* and *Frankenstein*, both with Udo Kier.

Wakefield Poole Poole revolutionized gay pornography and elevated it to high art—and therefore into a wider underground sphere than just gay—with his films *Boys in the Sand* (1971), *Bijou* (1972), and *Take One* (1977).

Jack Smith Underground director whose work was most associated with camp and trash and is often contrasted with Andy Warhol, although they come from the same era. Most famous for his experimental 1963 film *Flaming Creatures*, a tribute to actor Maria Montez.

Andy Warhol Everyone knows who Andy Warhol is.

SELECTED ZINES

Anonymous Boy Tony Arena's *Anonymous Boy* comics began as a regular feature in *J.D.s*, a sort of gay-male counterpoint to G.B. Jones's Tom Girls illustrations. Its teen-punk heroes are tough but sweet, crudely drawn but surprisingly sexy—and the sex is explicit and pervasive. Arena's single-panel comics were released in several collections throughout the 1990s and '00s, and an animated film titled *Green Pubes* was released in 1996, considered the first (and only) animated queer-core film. Arena was also a regular columnist for *Maximum Rocknroll*.

Bimbox/S.C.A.B. Sassy, surly, and constantly courting controversy, *Bimbox* was the spawn of Toronto hellraisers Johnny Noxzema and Rex Boy. From the late 1980s through the mid-1990s *Bimbox*, along with sister publication *S.C.A.B.* (*Society for the Complete Annihilations of Breeders*), challenged both gay and punk orthodoxies with scathing humor, and no one—from AIDS activists to unborn fetuses—was beyond the reach of their vitriol. As one reviewer described

Bimbox

S.C.A.B., "This is the most hateful thing I've ever seen in my life, and I kind of like it."

Chainsaw Published in the late 1980s and early '90s by Donna Dresch, *Chainsaw* served as a document of the West Coast scene, from the highly personal perspective of one of its great movers and shakers. At the time Dresch was playing in indie bands like Dinosaur Jr. and Screaming Trees, and her experiences as a woman in that male-dominated world informed much of her writing; the zine also featured contributions from G.B. Jones, Bruce LaBruce, Larry-Bob Roberts, and other heavy hitters from the queer publishing world. After three issues, *Chainsaw* morphed into a record label, and Dresch went on to form the seminal dyke band Team Dresch.

Double Bill Something of an all-star publication from Toronto's G.B. Jones, Jena von Brucker, Johnny Noxzema, Caroline Azar, and Rexboy, *Double Bill* took as its premise the juxtaposition of two very different celebrities named Bill: the beefy, mustachioed actor/ film producer William Conrad and junk-sick author and counterculture hero William S. Burroughs. Tongue only partly in cheek, the *Double Bill* crew spent ten years and five issues hammering away at the Burroughs

Double Bill

mystique, pitting his misogynist, bad-boy persona against the large, lovable Conrad. The long-running feminist takedown was featured in the *Village Voice*, nominated for Canada's Trillium Award, and made major waves in the world of queer zines.

Dr. Smith By some accounts, the One That Started It All. Published in mid-1980s Toronto, *Dr. Smith* was a major influence on G.B. Jones and Bruce LaBruce in creating their own epochal zine, *J.D.s*. Alongside the band interviews, detourned comics, and xerox collages characteristic of '80s punk zines, *Dr. Smith* also featured left-field queers like Warhol superstar Ondine and lesbian filmmaker Barbara Hammer. A spirited takedown of William Burroughs in the debut issue presaged the later Toronto zine *Double Bill*, which would make Burroughs-bashing its principal mission.

Dr. Smith

Factsheet Five Alongside *Maximum Rocknroll*, this long-running compendium of zine reviews played a crucial role in building networks and communities among queer zine publishers and like-minded readers. From its first appearance in 1982 through its final 1998 edition, *Factsheet Five* reviewed thousands of zines over sixty-four issues.

Fag School First published in Oakland in 2001, Brontez Purnell's *Fag School* played a big part in ushering the queercore aesthetic into the new millennium, featuring Brontez's hilarious and highly personal tales of life as a gay, black punk in early '00s San Francisco/Bay Area, alongside interviews, explicit photos, and a recurring advice column from Alison Wolfe of the band Bratmobile. Brontez has played in queer/punk bands such as Gravy Train!!! and The Younger Lovers and has published several books. He cofounded the Brontez Purnell Dance Company in 2010, now based in New York.

Fembot Published for three issues in the '90s—and two additional issues under the title *Fembot Presents Jam While You Cram*—Fembot's principal aim was to celebrate women in music, from the Shangri-Las to British queer-punk heroes Huggy Bear. Editor Gary Fembot has had a significant impact on queercore in the Bay Area for several decades as a member of the band Sta-Prest and a filmmaker working with artists like G.B. Jones and Brontez Purnell.

Fertile La Toyah Jackson Published out of LA by the legendary artist, performer, and pioneer of "terrorist drag" Vaginal Davis, *Fertile La Toyah Jackson* was like no other zine around. Described in the *Advocate* as "a veritable John Waters film of a skinny 'zine," it was dishy and exuberant, its look and tone having more in common with heartthrob rags like *Teen Beat* than with any punk zines of the day. In Fertile's world, rock stars and celebrities rubbed shoulders with drag queens and misfits—an A-list of "par-tay" invitees from issue no. 5 includes such disparate names as punk artist Alice Bag, gay activist Harry Hay, and action movie star Jean-Claude Van Damme. *Fertile La Toyah Jackson* was published throughout the '80s and early '90s, and a video edition of the zine was released in 1993.

HIDE was a pioneering multimedia zine published in the mid-1980s by Caroline Azar (of the band Fifth Column) and Candy Parker, with later help from G.B. Jones. Primarily a music zine, each issue was released with a cassette compilation of local/queer-minded bands and played a huge role in kickstarting Toronto's queercore scene. Jones has described *HIDE* as the "gateway" to her subsequent zine *J.D.s*.

Holy Titclamps Over an impressive fourteen years (1989–2003) and nineteen issues, *Holy Titclamps*, published in Minneapolis and San Francisco, chronicled, critiqued, and celebrated the queer punk scene more thoroughly than perhaps any other publication of the time, featuring prose, poetry, and visual art from stellar contributors like Robert Gluck, Sarah Schulman, and Michelle Tea. Editor Larry-Bob Roberts also extensively reviewed other queer zines for his long-running series *Queer Zine Explosion*. Larry-Bob maintains extensive archives online.

Homocore The budding scene's answer to *Maximum Rocknroll*, the long-running "punk bible" published monthly out of San Francisco, *Homocore* was cleanly and legibly typeset (by punk standards), and shared *MRR*'s basic formula: recurring columnists, music, and zine reviews and an extensive letters section that came to serve as a sort of social network for queer punks of the day. Eventually the zine was published on newsprint, with a print run of thousands, before editors Tom Jennings and Deke Nihilson called it quits in 1991.

Homocore

J.D.s was the brainchild of Toronto filmmakers, musicians, and raconteurs G.B. Jones and Bruce LaBruce, and was as close as queercore may have come to a defining document. Borrowing from Warhol and the Situationists, *J.D.s* imagineered a movement of queer punks that seemed to leap from its pages and into the streets. Within a decade of *J.D.s* inaugural 1985 issue, queer zines would number in the hundreds, if not thousands.

J.D.s

Little Caesar Dennis Cooper's *Little Caesar*, which he began publishing in late-70s Los Angeles, was more a literary mag than a straight-up zine, but its look and sensibility were punk through and through, with Patti Smith and Iggy Pop appearing alongside poets like John Weiners and future US laureate Billy Collins. Cooper later moved to New York and played a huge part in introducing the early queercore movement to the larger world through the pages of the *Village Voice*. Cooper is a celebrated novelist and elder statesman of experimental literature.

Maximum Rocknroll Not, by any standard, a queer zine—founder and long-time editor Tim Yohannon was known for harboring homophobic sentiments—*MRR* nonetheless played a pivotal role in the queer zine explosion of the late 1980s and the '90s. Through its lengthy letters section, zine and record reviews, and columnists such as Mykel Board and Mattilda Bernstein Sycamore, the monthly magazine, referred to by some as the "punk bible," has helped to spread the gospel of queer punk more widely than just about any other publication. Occasional all-queer issues highlighted a wide range of bands and figures from the scene.

Maximum Rocknroll, "The Absolutely Queer Issue"

Outpunk was a zine and record label run by San Francisco's Matt Wobensmith, a former writer for *Maximum Rocknroll*. With its first issue appearing in 1992, the zine in many ways picked up where *Homocore* left off when it ceased publication in 1991. Alongside big names like Tribe 8 and Pansy Division, *Outpunk* also celebrated lesser-known West Coast bands and artists such as Sta-Prest and Mukilteo Fairies.

Sister Nobody Close in spirit to Donna Dresch's *Chainsaw* (they also shared a mailing address in San Francisco), *Sister Nobody* was an early example of the "per-zine": highly personal, largely handwritten stories and reflections from editor Laura Sister Nobody on everything from Frida Kahlo and Sinead O'Connor, alongside contributions from kindred spirits such as G.B. Jones and Deke Nihilson. Two issues, published in the early '90s, helped inspire droves of women to take up self-publishing as a part of the queer zine explosion.

Straight to Hell Not strictly a queer-punk zine, *Straight to Hell* was started in the early 1970s by eccentric sex-enthusiast Boyd McDonald, and was largely comprised of cum-drenched, true-life stories submitted by readers, alongside Macdonald's wide-ranging cultural commentary. *Straight to Hell* was hugely influential, counting William Burroughs, Tennessee Williams, and Christopher Isherwood among its fans, and its stark graphics and no-apologies approach set the tone for the queer self-publishing scene that would blossom a decade later. It remains in publication under editor Billy Miller.

THING Among the many queer zines of the early '90s, *THING* was unique in both its aesthetic and focus. Started in 1989 by Chicago writer and activist Robert Ford (along with collaborators Trent Adkins and

Lawrence Warren), *THING* celebrated queer artists of color working in the margins and intersections of punk, drag, and performance, such as Vaginal Davis, Deee-Lite, and (pre-fame) RuPaul. More ambitious than most of its contemporaries, *THING* grew into an influential newsprint publication with a circulation of thousands. After ten issues, it ceased publication in 1993. Ford died in 1994.

This Is the Salivation Army Artist Scott Treleaven began publishing *This is the Salivation Army* in 1993 after the name and idea appeared to him in a dream: an army of queer lovers, moving in the shadows like a pack of wolves, would infiltrate and infuriate the civilized world, its ranks swelling as its exploits gained renown—almost a fable for the Toronto scene from which it emerged. In dialogue with queer mystics like Austin Osman Spare and Genesis P-Orridge, the zine articulated an occult vision of queer/punk existence that would continue to resonate well into the new millennium. Treleaven released a film with the same name in 2002, and a book-length anthology was published in 2006.

QUEERCORE ESSENTIAL RECORDS (CHRONOLOGICALLY)

Of course, you can always start with *J.D.s*'s rotating top-ten homocore list when it comes to music, but if that's not enough, strap these on for size.

Wayne County and The Electric Chairs, *Man Enough to Be a Woman*, 1978, Safari Records Jayne's *Man Enough to Be a Woman* packs queerness right into the title, although she was still going by Wayne County at the time, but with her transgender presentation front and center. County's music was always more traditional rock'n'roll than most of the other bands even by straight punk standards, but her love of it was pure and blasphemous, evidenced in jams "Rock & Roll Resurrection" and "Eddie & Sheena." But it was equally oozing with sex, including opening banger and classic "Fuck Off" and "Toilet Love" (these songs appear on the German version). The Canadian release had a completely different track list and included her own queer anthem: title track "Man Enough to Be a Woman."

Nervous Gender, *Music from Hell*, 1981, Subterranean Records Another example of "proto-queercore," Nervous Gender's name confronted the audience as much as Jayne County's album titles, but the music was decidedly more radical. Part of the early synth-punk movement that included the Screamers, Nervous Gender were confrontational, weird, and proudly perverse ("Bathroom Sluts"). The original lineup included "Jewish lesbian folk singer" Phranc, but she left before they released their one and only LP,

Music from Hell. Proof that punk and queers really wanted to rip it up and start again. Missing from the LP: single "Confession" in which singer Gerardo Velázquez proclaims, "Jesus was a cocksucking Jew, Jesus was just like me."

Fifth Column, *To Sir with Hate*, 1986, Hide *J.D.s* coeditor and filmmaker G.B. Jones along with Caroline Azar, Anita Smith, and Charlotte Briede probably delivered the definitive queercore musical statement of the 1980s. The band, whose name meant subversion from within, released their debut with not so much a three-chord thrash, but a post-punk middle finger, coupled with a great sense of humor, at heterosexist bourgeois culture right at the birth of queercore movement proper. Perhaps most famous on the album is "The Fairview Mall Story," which includes a prancy rap bridge with Bruce LaBruce.

Huggy Bear, *Taking the Rough with the Smooch*, 1993, Kill Rock Stars While queercore primarily seemed (at first) a North American phenomenon, things were brewing on the other side of the Atlantic and that included Huggy Bear, introduced to scores of American kids through their split with Bikini Kill, *Our Troubled Youth*. Don't be fooled by the cuddly name . . . their sound was as searing as it comes, and their collection of EPs, *Taking the Rough with the Smooch*, delivered some of the 1990s best tracks on homosexuality ("Pansy Twist") and teenage gender revolution ("Herjazz"), among others.

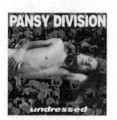

Pansy Division, *Undressed*, 1993, Lookout! Records If you already know Pansy Division, picking up any record would suffice as their best, but before anyone knew who they were, their 1993 debut made waves as the first over(gay)sexed pop-punk record in existence. *Undressed*, including songs "Bunnies," "Fem in a Black Leather Jacket," "The Cocksucker Club," and a gay take on The Ramones' "Rock 'n' Roll High School," set the stage for an entire career of tongue-in-check, funny, and thoroughly poppy punk for the 1990s and beyond.

Sister George, *Drag King*, 1994, Catcall Huggy Bear weren't alone in the UK in championing queercore in the 1990s. Sister George took their name from the 1968 lesbian dramedy *The Killing of Sister George*. Their only album *Drag King* was pure abrasive punk with a queer attack on heteronormative society, mixed with pop culture soundbites. The album included a cover of Tom Robinson's "Glad to Be Gay" renamed "100 X No!" with samples of Aileen Wuornos.

Various artists, *Outpunk Dance Party*, 1994, Outpunk Matt Wobensmith's Outpunk Records was one of the most prolific disseminators of the musical queer(core) agenda of all time and it was also the first. Wobensmith ran the zine of the same name, as well as wrote a column for *Maximum Rocknroll*, but his label put many queercore acts out that may have not had a chance for exposure otherwise and flourished because of it. *Outpunk Dance Party* was the sampler that introduced many kids to bands like Sister George, CWA, Pansy Division, Tribe 8, and more. It also included an intro from a pre–*Drag Race* RuPaul.

Tribe 8, *Fist City*, 1995, Alternative Tentacles Tribe 8 could mean fucking business and make you split your sides at the same time while doing it. Their debut, fittingly called *Fist City*, featured a kick-ass black warrior woman on the front and was a gauntlet thrown down at straight culture. At the same time, the back featured the band alternately holding flowers or switchblades. The record was pure punk rock, proud homo assault, with "Femme Bitch Top" being the anthemic cherry on top for deviant sex-positive dykes that were more Black Flag than black tea.

Team Dresch, *Personal Best*, 1995, Candy Ass/Chainsaw Records Parallel to Tribe 8 pounding their way into the scene, Team Dresch delivered an equally blistering debut, named for the 1982 Mariel Hemingway lesbian sports drama. While more melodic than *Fist City*, its politics were tattooed just as brazenly on its arm with the first two tracks "Fagetarian and Dyke" and "Hate the Christian Right."

The music was unmistakably hard but tempered by vocal melodies that could be sweet and screamy at the same time. The band was named for Donna Dresch, but Jody Bleyle, Marcéo Martinez, and Kaia Wilson stood out just as much making Team Dresch the Pacific Northwest's united dyke front.

The Third Sex, *Card Carryin'*, 1996, Chainsaw Records The Third Sex straddled the line between riot grrrl and queercore, riding both movements' simultaneous wave. The trio's similarities to both Sleater-Kinney and 7 Year Bitch were unmistakable, and they toured with both Bikini Kill and Bratmobile. But both the band name (among other meanings, the concept that homosexuals are neither male nor female but occupy a third sex or gender) and the title of the record loudly proclaimed them as queer (or worse than . . .). The Third Sex broke up in 2000, but their lightning fast licks and pretty-to-screamy vocal melodies could have pushed them along the same trajectory as another Portland trio, if that's what they wanted.

God Is My Co-Pilot, *The Best of God Is My Co-Pilot*, 1996, Atavistic Records GIMCP are prolific, not for one particular album but their output. Typically lo-fi and minimal, the band put out eleven records in their seven-year career (and numerous singles), all with at least over two dozen songs (until their last), all on independent labels and most songs under two minutes. Their best of was released only three years after their debut—that's how much material they had. Really, picking up any record by the hardworking queers works, but their *Best of* is the surefire way to get a super appropriate cover of The Fall's "Totally Wired" and their unbeatable "QDA (Anthem)," a sizzling hot, almost dance jam that includes the refrain "We're here, we're queer, we're gonna fuck your children."

Cypher in the Snow, *Blow Away the Glitter Diamonds from the Crown*, 1997, Candy Ass Records Cypher really gets two awards here. One for the killer LP and one for perhaps the most queer-punk 7" cover of all fucking time: "Badass and Free." The debut of the all-dyke queercore ensemble featured Blatz and Gr'ups alumna Anna Joy Springer, future *L-Word* actor Daniela Sea, and many, many others. They come off as a ragtag gang of queercore street urchins with an agenda to kick ass by orchestrating a circus of castration and middle fingers at Middle America. Hell, the refrain of their opening song "Militia" contains the line: "Kick ass with the girls' militia. Smashing patriarchy is what we're about—kill 'em all and let the goddess sort 'em out."

Peaches, *The Teaches of Peaches*, 2000, Kitty Yo Even though Peaches' first record was more beats and raps than three-chord rock (although there's that in there, too), her contemporary Chilly Gonzales once said that punk rock was Peaches's thing. And he wasn't wrong. *The Teaches of Peaches* blasted onto the underground music scene with enough attitude to knock the best rockers out. "Fuck the Pain Away," "Lovertits," and "Set It Off" were sexually charged minimal electro raps that put unrestrained sex front and center of queer discourse once again, and they remain classics to this day. Hell, the whole record does. Peaches herself hasn't gone anywhere either, only getting queerer and weirder as time went on.

Le Tigre, *Feminist Sweepstakes*, 2001, Mr. Lady Kathleen Hanna's electroclash project's sophomore effort basically opens with "For the ladies and the fags, yeah, we're the band with the roller-skate jams." It has to be said that Le Tigre's first record may hold a higher spot in the musical canon, but it was JD Samson's addition to Hanna and Johanna Fateman, as well as some specifically queer anthemic tracks, that put this one on the list. Samson added an element of charismatic lesbian visibility to the band and songs like the aforementioned "LT Tour Theme" and the incredibly powerful "Keep on Living" made *Feminist Sweepstakes* just a shade queerer. And in the end, it's just as much a perfect collection of electro-dance music with a fierce punk rock attitude underneath as the first.

Various artists, *Stand Up + Fucking Fight for It Queers in Hardcore + Punk*, 2002, Agitprop! Records Coming out at a time when most queercore was moving in an electro direction, Agitprop's—the label themselves inspired by Outpunk Records—compilation was another reminder of the roots of queercore and that while everyone was slathered in funky sexuality, there was still plenty of room and reason to be angry. Highlights: The Haggard, Fagatron, Scott Free, Skinjobs.

Gravy Train!!!!, *Hello Doctor*, 2003, Kill Rock Stars As the hard thrashing of 1990s queercore gave way to the electropunk synths and beats of the early 2000, there wasn't a band that better represented the collision of underground queer, punk sensibilities and a campy appreciation of dance better than Gravy Train!!!! Chunx, Funx, Hunx, and Drunx (later replaced by Junx aka Brontez Purnell) were like if a Saturday morning cartoon had sex with a John Waters–penned romance novel. Their debut record was a bubbly confection of obnoxious shrieks and singalong raps delivering gems like "You Made Me Gay," "Hella Nervous," and "Titties Bounce." Their subsequent records retained the fun but the glee on *Hello Doctor* remains unmatched.

Limp Wrist, *Complete Discography*, 2004, Lengua Armada Discos By the time Limp Wrist's debut came around, queercore as a concept had been kicking around for about fifteen years. It's all the more surprising that there's no comparable hardcore band that dealt explicitly with gay male issues. Jackhammer songs that come in under two minutes, lyrics that either espouse man-on-man love or hate for mainstream society/religion, and a feeling that queer people had some truly rage-cathartic music in the 2000s made Limp Wrist the lavender standard for queer punk rock (in the strictest sense) in the first decade of the 2000s. The complete discography includes the debut and a slew of hot singles. Highlights: "I Love Hardcore Boys/I Love Boys Hardcore," "Limp Wrist V. Dr. Laura," and "Does Your Daddy Know?"

Gossip, *Standing in the Way of Control*, 2006 (Kill Rock Stars) The thoroughly groovy blues punk of Gossip had already been going for two superb underground records—*That's Not What I Heard* and *Movement*—carried by Beth Ditto's incomparable Southern pipes and Brace Paine's shaking riffs, but if Gossip were Blondie, *Standing in the Way of Control* would be their *Parallel Lines*, albeit with a more coherent sound. At once punk rock and thoroughly danceable, with the addition of Hannah Blilie on drums and queer themes front and center yet somehow universal, *Standing* was a breakthrough and a huge smash in Europe. While it took America time to catch up, every queer in the rest of the Western Hemisphere was dancing to *Standing* in 2006.

G.L.O.S.S., *Trans Day of Revenge*, 2016, Total Negativity/Nervous Nelly/Pansy Twist distro/ Sabotage The most contemporary record on this list is also its shortest coming in at just under seven minutes. But its brevity isn't the point. Olympia-based G.L.O.S.S. (Girls Living Outside Society's Shit) breathed new life into queers playing hardcore—and we mean hard. Their only "record," *Trans Day of Revenge*, opens with "Give Violence a Chance" and hammers a nail into straight white scene and heteronormative culture that permeates everyday life. Their record is still available through Bandcamp, with proceeds going toward Olympia homeless shelter Interfaiths Works Emergency Overnight Shelter. G.L.O.S.S. even turned down a major deal from Epitaph Records before breaking up after only a two-year run.

ABOUT THE EDITORS

Liam Warfield is a writer, editor, and educator living in Chicago.

Walter Crasshole is a journalist in Berlin and English-language editor for the city's forty-year-running queer magazine *Siegessäule*. He is also a regular contributor and columnist for *Exberliner*, Berlin's English-language magazine, covering queer and cultural topics. He occasionally translates books from German to English, having just finished his third book translation for punk performance artist Wolfgang Müller.

Yony Leyser grew up in Chicago and relocated to Berlin in 2010. He is the writer and director of three award-winning feature films: *William S. Burroughs: A Man Within*; *Desire Will Set You Free*; and *Queercore: How to Punk a Revolution*. He has received critical acclaim in publications such as the *New York Times*, the *Guardian, Sight and Sound*, and the *Los Angeles Times*.

ABOUT PM PRESS

PM Press is an independent, radical publisher of books and media to educate, entertain, and inspire. Founded in 2007 by a small group of people with decades of publishing, media, and organizing experience, PM Press amplifies the voices of radical authors, artists, and activists. Our aim is to deliver bold political ideas and vital stories to all walks of life and arm the dreamers to demand the impossible. We have sold millions of copies of our books, most often one at a time, face to face. We're old enough to know what we're doing and young enough to know what's at stake. Join us to create a better world.

PM Press
PO Box 23912
Oakland, CA 94623
www.pmpress.org

PM Press in Europe
europe@pmpress.org
www.pmpress.org.uk

FRIENDS OF PM PRESS

These are indisputably momentous times—the financial system is melting down globally and the Empire is stumbling. Now more than ever there is a vital need for radical ideas.

In the years since its founding—and on a mere shoestring— PM Press has risen to the formidable challenge of publishing and distributing knowledge and entertainment for the struggles ahead. With over 450 releases to date, we have published an impressive and stimulating array of literature, art, music, politics, and culture. Using every available medium, we've succeeded in connecting those hungry for ideas and information to those putting them into practice.

Friends of PM allows you to directly help impact, amplify, and revitalize the discourse and actions of radical writers, filmmakers, and artists. It provides us with a stable foundation from which we can build upon our early successes and provides a much-needed subsidy for the materials that can't necessarily pay their own way. You can help make that happen—and receive every new title automatically delivered to your door once a month—by joining as a Friend of PM Press. And, we'll throw in a free T-shirt when you sign up.

Here are your options:

- **$30 a month** Get all books and pamphlets plus 50% discount on all webstore purchases

- **$40 a month** Get all PM Press releases (including CDs and DVDs) plus 50% discount on all webstore purchases

- **$100 a month** Superstar—Everything plus PM merchandise, free downloads, and 50% discount on all webstore purchases

For those who can't afford $30 or more a month, we have **Sustainer Rates** at $15, $10, and $5. Sustainers get a free PM Press T-shirt and a 50% discount on all purchases from our website.

Your Visa or Mastercard will be billed once a month, until you tell us to stop. Or until our efforts succeed in bringing the revolution around. Or the financial meltdown of Capital makes plastic redundant. Whichever comes first.

Punk Rock: An Oral History

John Robb
with a foreword by Henry Rollins

ISBN: 978-1-60486-005-4
$19.95   584 pages

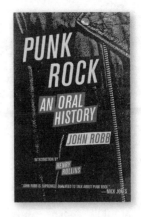

With its own fashion, culture, and chaotic energy, punk rock boasted a do-it-yourself ethos that allowed anyone to take part. Vibrant and volatile, the punk scene left an extraordinary legacy of music and cultural change. John Robb talks to many of those who cultivated the movement, such as John Lydon, Lemmy, Siouxsie Sioux, Mick Jones, Chrissie Hynde, Malcolm McLaren, Henry Rollins, and Glen Matlock, weaving together their accounts to create a raw and unprecedented oral history of UK punk. All the main players are here: from The Clash to Crass, from The Sex Pistols to the Stranglers, from the UK Subs to Buzzcocks—over 150 interviews capture the excitement of the most thrilling wave of rock 'n' roll pop culture ever. Ranging from its widely debated roots in the late 1960s to its enduring influence on the bands, fashion, and culture of today, this history brings to life the energy and the anarchy as no other book has done.

"Its unique brand of energy helps make it a riot all its own."
—*Harp* magazine

"John Robb is a great writer . . . and he is supremely qualified in my opinion to talk about punk rock."
—Mick Jones, The Clash

"John Robb is as punk rock as The Clash."
—Alan McGee

Bodies and Barriers: Queer Activists on Health

Adrian Shanker with a Foreword by
Rachel L. Levine, MD and an Afterword by
Kate Kendell

ISBN: 978-1-62963-784-6
$20.00   256 pages

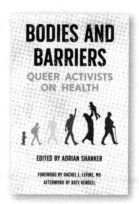

LGBT people pervasively experience health disparities,
affecting every part of their bodies and lives. Yet many
are still grappling to understand the mutually reinforcing health care challenges
that lead to worsened health outcomes. *Bodies and Barriers* informs health care
professionals, students in health professions, policymakers, and fellow activists
about these challenges, providing insights and a road map for action that could
improve queer health.

Through artfully articulated, data-informed essays by twenty-six well-known and
emerging queer activists—including Alisa Bowman, Jack Harrison-Quintana, Liz
Margolies, Robyn Ochs, Sean Strub, Justin Sabia-Tanis, Ryan Thoreson, Imani
Woody, and more—*Bodies and Barriers* illuminates the health challenges LGBT
people experience throughout their lives and challenges conventional wisdom
about health care delivery. It probes deeply into the roots of the disparities faced
by those in the LGBT community and provides crucial information to fight for
health equity and better health outcomes.

The contributors to *Bodies and Barriers* look for tangible improvements, drawing
from the history of HIV/AIDS in the U.S. and from struggles against health care
bias and discrimination. At a galvanizing moment when LGBT people have
experienced great strides in lived equality, but our health as a community still lags,
here is an indispensable blueprint for change by some of the most passionate and
important health activists in the LGBT movement today.

"Now, more than ever, we need Bodies and Barriers *to shine a spotlight on how and
why good healthcare for LGBTQ people and our families is such a challenge.* Bodies
and Barriers *provides a road map for all who are ready to fight for health equity—in
the doctor's office, in the halls of government, or in the streets."*
—Rea Carey, executive director, National LGBTQ Task Force

*"*Bodies and Barriers *helps LGBT community members understand the way people in
the U.S. health services market erect barriers to anyone who is not the source of easy
and immediate profit, and helps us all confront and break down these barriers. It helps
families of LGBT people understand these obstacles and options for getting around
them. And it helps health professionals hear the voices of all their patients, so that we
learn to listen, and learn how to care for everyone."*
—Michael Fine, MD, former director, Rhode Island Department of Health, author
of *Health Care Revolt: How to Organize, Build a Health Care System, and Resuscitate
Democracy All at the Same Time*

One Chord Wonders: Power and Meaning in Punk Rock

Dave Laing
with a Foreword by TV Smith

ISBN: 978-1-62963-033-5
$17.95   224 pages

Originally published in 1985, *One Chord Wonders* was the first full-length study of the glory years of British punk rock. The book argues that one of punk's most significant political achievements was to expose the operations of power in the British entertainment industries as they were thrown into confusion by the sound and the fury of musicians and fans.

Through a detailed examination of the conditions under which punk emerged and then declined, Dave Laing develops a view of the music as both complex and contradictory. Special attention is paid to the relationship between punk and the music industry of the late 1970s, in particular the political economy of the independent record companies through which much of punk was distributed. The rise of punk is also linked to the febrile political atmosphere of Britain in the mid-1970s.

Using examples from a wide range of bands, individual chapters use the techniques of semiology to consider the radical approach to naming in punk (from Johnny Rotten to Poly Styrene), the instrumental and vocal sound of the music, and its visual images. Another section analyses the influence of British punk in Europe prior to the music's division into "real punk" and "post-punk" genres.

The concluding chapter critically examines various theoretical explanations of the punk phenomenon, including the class origins of its protagonists and the influential view that punk represented the latest in a line of British youth "subcultures." There is also a chronology of the punk era, plus discographies and a bibliography.

"A clear, unprejudiced account of a difficult subject."
—Jon Savage, author of *England's Dreaming*

Girls Will Be Boys Will Be Girls Will Be . . . Coloring Book

Jacinta Bunnell

ISBN: 978-1-62963-507-1
$11.00   40 pages

This updated edition of the iconic coloring book *Girls Will Be Boys Will Be Girls Will Be . . .* by Jacinta Bunnell contains all new illustrations and questions for contemplation. In this groundbreaking coloring book, you will meet girls who build drum sets and fix bikes, boys who bake and knit, and all manner of children along the gender spectrum. Children are tender, vulnerable, tough, zany, courageous, and gentle, no matter what their gender. This coloring book is for all the heroic handsome beauties of the world and for everyone who has ever colored outside the lines—a reminder that we never need to compromise ourselves to fit someone else's idea of who we ought to be.

Featuring illustrations by Giselle Potter, Nicole Georges, Kristine Virsis, Simi Stone, Jacinta Bunnell, Nicole Rodrigues, Richard Wentworth, and many more, this is the perfect book for the gender creative person in your life. The future is gender fabulous.

"*A perfect alternative to gender-saturated Disney fare.*"
—*Bitch* magazine

"*A great inexpensive gift for kids age 5 to 95.*"
—*Curve* magazine

"*If I had had this coloring book when I was little, I think things would have been a little easier for me, and when you're little a little easier is a lot.*"
—Lynda Barry, cartoonist

The Spitboy Rule: Tales of a Xicana in a Female Punk Band

Michelle Cruz Gonzales with a Foreword by Martín Sorrondeguy and Preface by Mimi Thi Nguyen

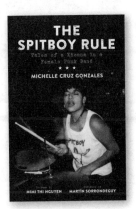

ISBN: 978-1-62963-140-0
$15.95   160 pages

Michelle Cruz Gonzales played drums and wrote lyrics in the influential 1990s female hardcore band Spitboy, and now she's written a book—a punk rock herstory. Though not a riot grrl band, Spitboy blazed trails for women musicians in the San Francisco Bay Area and beyond, but it wasn't easy. Misogyny, sexism, abusive fans, class and color blindness, and all-out racism were foes, especially for Gonzales, a Xicana and the only person of color in the band.

Unlike touring rock bands before them, the unapologetically feminist Spitboy preferred Scrabble games between shows rather than sex and drugs, and they were not the angry manhaters that many expected them to be. Serious about women's issues and being the band that they themselves wanted to hear, a band that rocked as hard as men but sounded like women, Spitboy released several records and toured internationally. The memoir details these travels while chronicling Spitboy's successes and failures, and for Gonzales, discovering her own identity along the way.

Fully illustrated with rare photos and flyers from the punk rock underground, this fast-paced, first-person recollection is populated by scenesters and musical allies from the time including Econochrist, Paxston Quiggly, Neurosis, Los Crudos, Aaron Cometbus, Pete the Roadie, Green Day, Fugazi, and Kamala and the Karnivores.

"The Spitboy Rule *is a compelling and insightful journey into the world of '90s punk as seen through the eyes of a Xicana drummer who goes by the nickname Todd. Todd stirs the pot by insisting that she plays hardcore punk, not Riot Grrrl music, and inviting males to share the dance floor with women in a respectful way. This drummer never misses a beat. Read it!"*
—Alice Bag, singer for the Bags, author of *Violence Girl: East L.A. Rage to Hollywood Stage, a Chicana Punk Story*

"*Incisive and inspiring, Michelle Cruz Gonzales's* The Spitboy Rule *brings the '90s punk world to life with equal parts heart and realism. Her story becomes a voyage of self-discovery, and Gonzales is the perfect guide—as she writes in rapidfire drum beats about epic road tours, female camaraderie, sexist fans, and getting accused of appropriating her own culture.*"
—Ariel Gore, *Hip Mama*

Going Underground: American Punk 1979–1989, *Second Edition*

George Hurchalla

ISBN: 978-1-62963-113-4

$21.95   416 pages

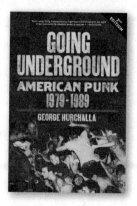

The product of decades of work and multiple self-published editions, *Going Underground*, written by 1980s scene veteran George Hurchalla, is the most comprehensive look yet at America's nationwide underground punk scene.

Despite the mainstream press declarations that "punk died with Sid Vicious" or that "punk was reborn with Nirvana," author Hurchalla followed the DIY spirit of punk underground, where it not only survived but thrived nationally as a self-sustaining grassroots movement rooted in seedy clubs, rented fire halls, Xeroxed zines, and indie record shops.

Rather than dwell solely on well-documented scenes from Los Angeles, New York, and Washington, DC, Hurchalla delves deep into the counterculture, rooting out stories from Chicago, Philadelphia, Austin, Cincinnati, Miami, and elsewhere. The author seamlessly mixes his personal experiences with the oral history of dozens of band members, promoters, artists, zinesters, and scenesters. Some of the countless bands covered include Articles of Faith, Big Boys, Necros, Hüsker Dü, Bad Brains, Government Issue, and Minutemen, as well as many of the essential zines of the time such as *Big Takeover*, *Maximum RocknRoll*, *Flipside*, and *Forced Exposure*.

Going Underground features over a hundred unique photos from Marie Kanger-Born of Chicago, Dixon Coulbourn of Austin, Brian Trudell of LA, Malcolm Riviera of DC, Justina Davies of New York, Ed Arnaud of Arizona, and many others, along with flyers from across the nation.

"Hurchalla's efforts are impressive, given the fragmented and regional nature of American hardcore in the Eighties, a time well before the Web made for a truly Punk Planet. Mimicking an Eighties-era tour, it meanders all over the place without ever fully wearing out its welcome."
—Marc Savlov, *Austin Chronicle*

"Chapter by chapter, Hurchalla captures each major cities' contribution, with the formation and rise of seminal clubs, bands, and indie record labels, all told through the anecdotes of the musicians, club promoters, zine publishers and scenesters themselves. Peppered with original show flyers and rare photographs, this anthropological perfect storm might leave latter-day punks thirsty at the trough, as baby, those were truly the golden years."
—John James, *Cincinnati CityBeat*

Praise for *Queercore*

"Finally, a book that centers on the wild, innovative, and fearless contributions queers made to punk rock, creating a punker-than-punk subculture beneath the subculture, queercore. Gossipy and inspiring, a historical document and a call to arms during a time when the entire planet could use a dose of queer, creative rage."
—Michelle Tea, author of *Valencia*

"I knew at an early age I didn't want to be part of a church; I wanted to be part of a circus. It's documents such as this book that give hope for our future. Anarchists, the queer community, the roots of punk, the Situationists, and all the other influential artistic guts eventually had to intersect. Queercore is completely logical, relevant, and badass."
—Justin Pearson, The Locust, Three One G

"This is a sensational set of oral histories of queer punk that includes everyone from Jayne County to Eileen Myles, from Vaginal Davis to Lynn Breedlove. The whole book works like a giant jigsaw puzzle that never offers a final or complete picture but at least scatters the pieces around to allow the reader to assemble some truly exciting scenarios. This is very possibly the best and only way that subcultural histories should emerge—namely as incomplete and incoherent, as a magnificent poly-vocal roar, as sound, fury, rebel yells and screams. This does not just capture queer punk; it *is* queer punk."
—Jack Halberstam, author of *The Queer Art of Failure* and *In a Queer Time and Place: Transgender Bodies, Subcultural Lives*

"*Queercore: How to Punk a Revolution* delivers a deeply invested history of the forgotten roots of queercore. While to some punk was inherently gay as fuck, the actual queer revolution came few and far between bands, scenes, and eras whose intersections were small, yet wildly significant. With voices ranging from Penny Arcade to Brontez Purnell, we hear a vast history from around the globe, echoing everything queer, dirty, and true."
—Cristy C. Road, frontwoman of Choked Up and author of *Spit and Passion* and *Next World Tarot*

"*Queercore* is the unrelenting polyrhythm of a culture, chanted in varied waves of sensation, by some of its most essential voices. Zigzagging through generations of nostalgia and controversy faster than their own power chords, this is not just a record of queercore (the movement), but a theoretical discussion about the intersectional ideology of 'queer,' as well as 'punk' itself. Reading—not watching or listening to—this book gave me the absolutely necessary opportunity to reinvigorate my own punk, both as performance art and radical protest. This unflinching oral history of how a subculture begins and survives, tenaciously layered in the present, is a bridge over the gap, that I, for one, have been waiting for."
—JD Samson, musician, producer, songwriter and DJ (Le Tigre/MEN)